```
D1453395
```

Too Busy To Die

Like other successful endeavors in my life, I credit my old friend, Mel Brooks… he always gives me sage advice. When I told him that I was at loose ends since completing my last book, "Carl Reiner, Now You're Ninety-Four," he shouted, "Start a new one and call it, 'Too Busy To Die.'" I thought it a smashing title, and hopefully "Too Busy To Die" will also turn out to be a smashing read.

Too Busy To Die

by

Carl Reiner

**RANDOM
CONTENT**
PUBLISHING

RANDOM CONTENT™
Beverly Hills, CA 90210
www.randomcontent.com

Published by RANDOM CONTENT 03/20/17

ISBN: 978-0-9915368-9-4

Library of Congress Control Number: 2017932352

Front cover photo by David Pascal
Back cover photo by White House Photographer

Any people depicted in images have given approval by their estate and trustees.

This book is printed on acid-free paper.

Because of the dynamic nature of the Internet, any web addresses or links contained in this book may have changed since publication and may no longer be valid.

Printed and bound in India by Replika Press Pvt. Ltd.

"Self-Plagiarism is the sincerest form of egotism."

Carl Reiner 2015

Contents

Judd Apatow   Me

Foreword

I was born in 1967 and have never known a moment on Earth when Carl Reiner was not giving me some sort of comedic gift. It started with "The Dick Van Dyke Show." It was warm and hilarious and introduced me to a world I dreamed of entering, that of the comedy writer. I am going to tell you a secret: my entire life has been a sad attempt at replicating Carl Reiner's life. He performed, so I started performing. He worked at a sketch show, so I worked at a sketch show. He wrote movies, so I wrote movies. He directed, so I directed. He was married to an incredibly talented woman who was also in show business, so I did the same. His son is a great actor, so I forced my two daughters to be actresses against their will. He fought in World War Two. I was not able to copy him there. He is creative well into his nineties. I am quickly losing my touch before hitting fifty.

So it has been a lifetime of wanting to be Carl. In addition to being a brilliant comedic mind, he is a wonderful person who I feel honored to have gotten to know a little bit over the years. Mel Brooks and Carl Reiner are best friends and see each other almost every night and watch TV. Sometimes I fantasize about sitting watching TV with them.

I may never get to fulfill that dream but I am honored to have had a great time reading this book and here's to a dozen more.

–Judd Apatow
Los Angeles

CHAPTER ONE

The Tuxedo and The B.C. Bow Tie
(Before Clip-ons)

Last evening, after having a sensible dinner with my friend Mel Brooks, I rummaged through a carton of DVD's and found an old classic film, "The Scoundrel." It was filmed in 1939 and starred Noel Coward, a multi-talented giant in the entertainment world. In his eighty-three years on earth, he wrote and starred in dozens of popular stage plays, composed the music, lyrics and librettos for musical comedies, revues and major motion pictures, playing leading roles in many of them.

While watching "The Scoundrel," Mel commented on how dexterously the tuxedo-clad Noel Coward had perfectly knotted his black bow-tie which, until the advent of the clip-on, was a rather difficult thing to do.

It was then I told Mel about how, at a formal Director's Guild awards dinner, because I wore a hand-knotted bow tie, I received the longest and loudest sustained laugh in my twenty five years as host.

Noel Coward

It started after I was introduced by Arthur Hiller, the Guild's president. As we stood at the podium, I mentioned that Arthur and I were both directors and asked if the bow tie he was wearing was a clip-on. He said it was and I said mine was not and undid it. I explained that most actors can tie a bow tie and most directors can't. To prove my point, I asked the audience of directors to raise their hands if they wore a clip-on. A sea of hands shot up and I explained that the reason I can tie mine is that, at seventeen, I played a dashing gigolo in "The Bishop Misbehaves." As I re-knotted my tie, I explained how for ten dollars I had bought a pair of formal tails and the clothing store clerk taught me how to knot a tie. I received a rather healthy applause, way beyond what my little tale deserved.

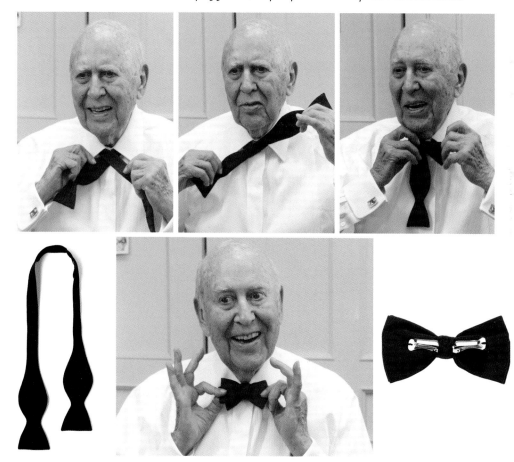

It never occurred to me that while I was talking, the 'clip-on tied' directors were applauding my ability to re-knot my tie without even looking into a mirror. For those who wished to learn how, I suggested that it was very much like tying your shoelace.

CHAPTER TWO

My Premier Performance

I made my initial stage appearance eighty-eight years ago when I was six. My first grade teacher cast me to play a role in the children's classic, "Six Who Pass While the Lentils Boil," which I performed at Public School 92. When the play ended, my mother, who was seated next to the school's Principal said to her, "That boy who played the Headsman was the best one."

Throughout my career my Mom would repeat the Principal's words, "Carl, you were the best one!" When I appeared on NBC's "Your Show of Shows," my Mom continued to tell me that I was "the best one," ofttimes adding "but they should give you more to do!"

Howard Morris

Sid Caesar

Imogene Coca

The Best One

CHAPTER THREE

My Ten Year Dry Spell

After my successful performance in "Six Who Pass While the Lentils Boil," I went on to Junior High School 65, where I never set foot on stage. At fourteen, I attended Evander Childs High School.

Evander Childs High School on Gunhill Rd.

I had an interest in acting and the school had a Drama Club but I was too shy to apply for membership. I passed the Drama Club's door many times but did not have the guts to go in.

In my junior year, an opportunity arose that gave me a chance to prove I had what it takes to become an actor. Our English teacher had assigned everyone in the class to memorize and recite a monologue from one of Shakespeare's plays. I chose Romeo and Juliet's balcony scene. Over the weekend I learned my part and, in a very creditable British accent, recited it perfectly.

When our teacher asked who would like to recite their speech, three class members volunteered. They delivered their speeches and received positive reactions. I feared that if I deliver my offering with my Ronald Colman-ish accent that they would think I was a show-off or some kind of nut.

In my senior year when our music teacher, Mr. Raskin, asked for volunteers to represent our school in the city wide Spanish festival I had thought of volunteering. I loved to sing, often entertaining my buddies, belting out the aria "Vesti La Giubba," but I didn't have to volunteer. My best friend, Milton Langsam, volunteered for me by shouting my name.

Milton Langsam

On a bright Saturday afternoon, I and Ruth Kanarek, a girl with whom I would be singing a duet, boarded the subway for a long ride to Julia Richmond High School, where the festival was held. Ruth and I watched performers from other schools sing and dance way, way better than I ever could. I also learned that Ruth Kanarek could outsing them all. When it was our turn, she delivered a beautifully rendered selection, "El Relicario," and, after a well deserved round of applause, Mr. Raskin played the introduction to our song "Yo Soy El Pato"– ("I Am The Duck").

Our number had been choreographed for Ruth to move coyly about the stage while rejecting my advances. It was a mild offering and was getting little reaction until I decided to lighten my performance by walking like a duck–splaying my feet and waddling after her.

The audience laughed and applauded long enough for us to take three curtain calls.

When we left the school, rather than taking the subway home, our ecstatic group celebrated by chipping in for a taxi. I had but thirty-three cents and contributed all but three cents. When we arrived in the Bronx and someone suggested we celebrate with pastrami sandwiches and Cream sodas, I bowed out by saying I had a previous appointment.

One year later I had moved from the stage at Julia Richmond High School to a stage in an off, off, off Broadway Theater–a Summer Theater stage in Rochester, New York.

CHAPTER FOUR

The Crotona Park & The Portable Theater

For the first 14 years of my life, I found no compelling reason to venture forth from my home in the East Bronx, since my old neighborhood had everything I needed to sustain me. In Crotona Park there's a hill behind ball field No. 3, at Fulton Avenue and the Cross Bronx Expressway, that's perfect for snow days. It was on this steep, snow-covered incline where, on a terrifying downhill sleigh ride, I learned that I was borderline agoraphobic. Seven years later, in 1935, while sitting on one of the park's gentler slopes, I fantasized about becoming an actor.

During the depression-years, my buddies Shlermy, Mutty, Lenny, David, Marty, I and 2,000 others would claim a section of this grassy slope and watch a colorfully painted truck roll in. Before our eyes the truck would drop its flaps and metamorphosize into a portable theater, replete with a proscenium, apron and wings.

During the mid-thirties the WPA funded a theater program employing thousands of out-of-work actors, directors, choreographers and scenic designers to bring joy to citizens who were hungry for entertainment. I remember sitting on the hill, waiting expectantly to see what this wonderful troupe had brought us this week. Some of the more affluent theatergoers would bring blankets to sit on, but our group opted to plop down on the dewy grass, accepting that we would go home with wet behinds.

While waiting for the play to begin, young entrepreneurs carrying brown paper bags, filled with pumpkin or sunflower seeds, snaked through the crowd shouting, "Get your nuts here!"

For a penny they would spill a shot glass full of seeds into your cupped hands.

My friend Mutty calculated that these young merchants were making a small fortune. They could buy a small bag of pumpkin seeds and, after

an evening of hawking their wares, could net as much as three bucks. It is within the realm of possibility that one of these enterprising lads now owns Whole Foods.

The first full length play I ever saw was "Friendly Enemies," and I remember how impressed I was with the brilliantly lit stage, the sets, the clarity of the actors' speech and how attractive were the young actresses. Resurfacing were the wonderful feelings I had when performing in "Six Who Pass While The Lentils Boil." In my last year of high school, I saw a full scale production of Gilbert and Sullivan's "The Mikado."

The costumes, the make-up, the singing, the sets and the orchestra, made my head spin. I thought the expression, "I could feel the hairs on my neck stand up," was just an expression but, this night, I actually felt my neck hairs rise.

The first rising happened when the chorus blended their voices to belt out the high notes at the end of the opening song, "If You Want to Know Who We Are." The second thrill came when Yum-Yum and her sisters sang, "Three Little Maids From School Are We."

The thrilling operatic voices of Peep-bo, Pitti Sing and Yum-Yum joining in harmony, again did its job on my neck hairs. I had fallen desperately in love with the beautiful singer who played Yum-Yum.

I was only 16 but, from the moment she peeked out from behind her fan and looked in my general direction, I knew that the theater was a good place to spend time.

Not long after, thanks to the our government sponsored Federal Theater Project, that opportunity presented itself.

CHAPTER FIVE

The WPA's Free Acting Classes

It was 1938, when our country was in the last year of a deep depression, President Franklin D. Roosevelt's WPA funded the training and sustaining of out-of-work bricklayers, bridge and road builders, fine artists, sculptors, musicians and yes, even actors.

I have written before of my brother Charlie, who always appreciated my ability to tell a joke or impersonate celebrities. When he was twenty and I seventeen, Charlie had read in the N.Y. Daily News that the WPA was offering free lessons for aspiring actors in downtown Manhattan at 100 Center Street. He clipped the article from the paper, handed it to me and insisted I "give it a shot."

My brother Charlie and me

W.P.A. Sponsored Theater Classes

The Federal Goverment's Works Project Administration has instituted a program that invites young men and women who are interested in Theater Arts to apply for admittance to one of their newly instituted programs. Aspiring actors wishing to apply may do so by appearing between 9AM & 5PM at 100 Center Street's Suite 49.

I heeded Charlie's advice, took the subway down to the imposing federal building at 100 Center Street and dared to register for a course in acting. A few years later I, again, entered this building, stood before a Justice of the Peace and married Estelle Lebost.

In a small classroom, I was welcomed by my first drama teacher, Mrs. Whitmore, a Grand Dame of the British theater. I shall never forget her first words, delivered with an impressive, resonant voice:

"Class, as your very first assignment, I ask you young men and women to memorize a particular speech from Shakespeare's "Romeo and Juliet." It is not one of the lovers' soliloquies but the speech that Queen Gertrude makes when describing the death of Ophelia."

For your reading pleasure, here now is that speech:

There is a willow grows aslant a brook,

That shows his hoar leaves in the glassy stream;

There with fantastic garlands did she come

Of crow-flowers, nettles, daisies, and long purples

That liberal shepherds give a grosser name,

But our cold maids do dead men's fingers call them:

There, on the pendent boughs her coronet weeds

Clambering to hang, an envious sliver broke;

When down her weedy trophies and herself

Fell in the weeping brook. Her clothes spread wide;

And, mermaid-like, awhile they bore her up:

Which time she chanted snatches of old tunes;

As one incapable of her own distress,

Or like a creature native and indued

Unto that element: but long it could not be

Till that her garments, heavy with their drink,

Pull'd the poor wretch from her melodious lay

To muddy death.

To this day, if I were awakened from a deep sleep and asked to deliver this speech, I would willingly oblige. I am forever beholden to Mrs. Whitmore for kick-starting my career.

One evening, a Mr. Jonas, an aspiring producer-director, visited our class looking for two actors to perform in a play he was preparing to mount. To read one of the play's love scenes he chose me and Barbara Comack. An unexpected and pleasant offshoot of that audition was my falling in love with beautiful Barbara Comack.

For a full year, until a fateful Sunday night, Barbara was my steady girl. One Sunday I had planned to take her to the Bronx Park Zoo and introduce her to all the animals I knew intimately, especially the llama who once thanked my brother for feeding him by spitting in his face.

I was on my way to pick her up when she phoned to say that a cousin from Connecticut was visiting and she could not get away. During the next few days, I called Barbara many times but was not able to reach her. She made no attempt to contact me and, to this day, I have no idea why I was dumped by someone who had allowed me to soul kiss her, touch her breasts and professed to love me.

Years later, after being hired for my first job in a summer theater, I sent her a letter telling her of my good fortune and received a post card back congratulating me... and nothing more.

That was seventy-seven years ago and to this day it remains a head-shaking mystery. I do wonder if Barbara Comack ever thought about the 'good catch' she had thrown back.

CHAPTER SIX

Gilmore vs. Weglinsky, Dueling Mentors

When I was seventeen I worked as a delivery boy for Abe Weglinsky, the owner of Weglinsky's Machine Shop. Mr. Weglinsky repaired millinery machines that were used to fashion ladies' straw and felt hats. The shop, which measured eight feet by twelve feet, was on the first floor of a narrow, turn-of-the-century, two story building that was located at 38th Street and 6th Avenue.

In that cramped area was a roll top desk, a tin-topped work bench that sported my boss' metal hand-drill, a vise, an assortment of files, clamps, hammers and sanding paper.

I delivered these small Willcox & Gibbs sewing machines that Mr. Weglinsky had repaired for his customers in the millinery trade.

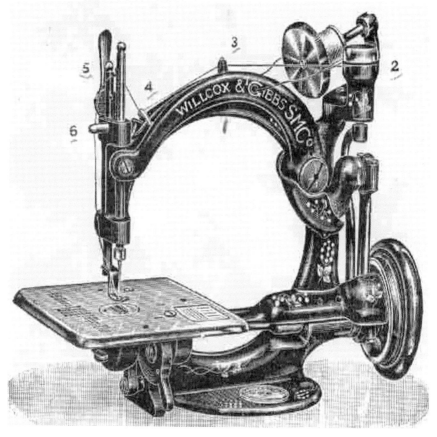

Each morning, I would arrive at 8 AM, climb atop the metal work bench, open the room's only window, sweep the eight by ten foot oil stained floor and empty the waste basket. Mr. Weglinsky paid me eight dollars a week, two of which I dutifully gave to my parents to help with household expenses. Miraculously, the six remaining dollars were enough to cover my subway fare to and from work and the nightly snack I had before pursuing my career in the theater.

One life changing day after delivering my last sewing machine, I hied to the 64th Street Cort Theater and gave my name to a grungy stage manager, who told me to join the young men who were waiting to audition.

It was there that I met Paul Gilmore, an imposing, grey haired thespian, and scion of the "Gilmore Free Theater."

Below is what Mr. Gilmore looked like 40 years earlier.

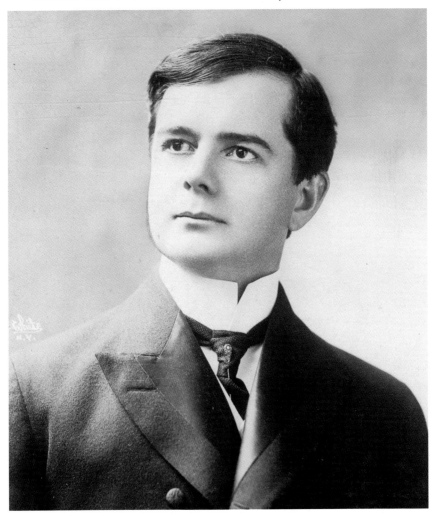

With a booming voice Mr. Gilmore asked me to state my name and a theater in which I had acted.

"Well, my name is Carl Reiner and it wasn't exactly a theater that I acted in."

"In what exactly was it?"

"It was a talent night, sir, in a big room at the James E. Murphy Democratic Club... in the Bronx... and I did impressions of Ronald Colman, Ed Wynn and Lou Holtz... and I also sang "The Isle of Capri."

For whatever reason, he didn't throw me out but told me to watch the show that night, "The Family Upstairs," and to pay attention to the actor who plays Willie Heller.

"That boy can not act," Mr. Gilmore explained, "and I am letting him go." Mr. Gilmore then handed me some yellowed pages and ordered, "Learn your lines and be ready to perform tomorrow night."

I scanned the part and I was happy to see that my role was a minor one. The next day, to and from work, while hanging onto a strap in the subway car, I managed to memorize the dozen lines.

I can vividly recall the fear that overcame me when I walked on stage for the first time—a fear that made my knees shake and my eyes cross. After delivering my first line cleanly and Paul Gilmore responding in character, my eyes uncrossed and, for the rest of the play, stayed uncrossed.

Paul Gilmore apparently had enough faith in my ability to cast me in his next production, "The Bishop Misbehaves," in which I would be playing Donald Meadows, a ne'er-do-well playboy.

It was a small but significant role where, before the final curtain, I delivered the last words of the play–eloquent words. In my best stage diction, I called for, "The cooperation of all nations to help bring everlasting peace to our troubled world."

The words and my performance were well received by the audience and especially my parents, who were there on opening night. Once again, my mother told me and everyone in earshot that I was the best one!

"The Bishop Misbehaves" was an audience favorite and ran six nights a week for one full year. I received no salary but was given a "scholarship" which Mr. Gilmore explained would ordinarily cost three to five dollars a week–the tuition he charged all of the aspiring actors of his drama school. After nine months of playing Donald Meadows for free, and depleting my eight dollar delivery boy salary by eating 30 cent dinners six days a week at Stewart's Cafeteria, I dared to ask Mr. Gilmore for a raise. One night, after a performance, I knocked on his dressing room door and asked to talk with him.

I told him that I could no longer afford to be in the play and he quickly reminded me that I was the only member of his acting school who was not paying tuition. I said that I appreciated that but, unless I was paid something, I would have to leave. It was then he allowed me to know just how well he thought of me.

"My boy," he said, reining in his booming voice, "because you have talent, I am going to do something I have never done before... if you promise to tell no one!"

I promised and, in 'sotto voce,' he offered to pay me a dollar.

"A dollar a performance!?" I asked gleefully.

"No, no, my boy! A dollar a week!"

This gracious raise was enough to keep me acting for him another three months before accepting a more lucrative job.

Actual Silver Certificate circa 1938

CHAPTER SEVEN

Summer Theater

While standing at a urinal in the lobby lavatory of the Gilmore Theater, a man using the adjacent urinal to me introduced himself to me as
Leslie Cutler. He praised my performance in "The Bishop Misbehaves,"
and asked if I had any interest in spending eight weeks as a member of
a summer theater company for which I would be paid room and board.
Every young actor's dream was getting a job at a summer theater and,
without a moments hesitation, I accepted his offer to become a member of "The Rochester Summer Theater." Two days later, after informing
Mr. Weglinsky I had to leave his employ, I was on a bus traveling upstate to
Avon, New York, where I would be given the opportunity to perform twelve
major and minor roles in twelve different plays. I was told I needed a white
gabardine suit for my first role and my Mom and I went shopping for it.
We found the one below that was priced at ten dollars, for which my Mom
offered a 'take-it-or-leave-it' seven dollars.

I folded my seven dollar suit into a used, five dollar Gladstone bag that Mom had bargained down from eight. The following morning, I found myself and my bag on a bus heading north.

While sitting in a window seat, and staring at the scenery, I started to learn lines for one of the leading roles in their first production, "The Three Cornered Moon." I was to play the part of Dr. Allen Evans. It was a long part and I worried that I might need more than a week to learn it.

By the time I alighted from the bus I had fairly well memorized three of the five scenes in which my character appeared.

At the Rochester bus station in Avon, New York, I was met by a young man who introduced himself as the company's stage manager. After tossing my "stuff" into the trunk of his dilapidated, wood-paneled station wagon, he told me, "Get in!" and we took off.

On the half-hour ride to the village, the driver volunteered a disquieting bit of news. He calmly informed me that before going to the boarding house, he would drop me off at the theater so I could rehearse with the cast for tomorrow's opening of "Three Cornered Moon," a popular Broadway play that had been adapted for a film. I panicked!

"Tomorrow night," I mumbled, "I've only learned the first two acts!"

The owner-director of "The Rochester Summer Theater," Leonard Altobell, was a short, dark haired, well-spoken man who, I soon learned, knew what he wanted and how to get it. When I informed him that I was not given time to learn all my lines, he informed me that the actor I was replacing, "knew all his lines but stunk up the stage!" Mr. Altobell assured me that there was no way I could be as bad.

When I complained that I had not yet memorized the last scene, he seemed delighted and assured me that if I burned a little midnight oil, by curtain time, I'd have that last scene under my belt.

At rehearsal, on the lawn adjacent to the outdoor theater, Mr. Altobell, in the foreground, conducted a rehearsal for the lead actors which included the blond, British accented Larry Slade and Margaret Whycherly, a famous German actress who fled the Nazis, came to America and found a small summer theater where she could work on losing her German accented speech.

After rehearsal Mr. Altobell advised me to keep studying, and then had someone drive me to the rooming house. Lying on a canvas cot on the third floor of an 'in need-of repair' rooming house, I stayed up most of the night. I read my lines from the script, then closed my eyes and quietly said them over and over again until I had fairly well memorized two of my three scenes.

It was during rehearsal that I came upon a possible solution for that unmemorized scene. Since I was playing a doctor, I decided to carry what could be a medical book. I'd place the play's pages in it and pretend to be reading the book.

When I heard my cue, I would casually look up, say my line, look down at the book and then learn my next line. I kept my focus on the book even during the first two acts, whose lines I had learned.

That all took place over seventy-years ago, but that night, the audience's applause and the words that a very pleased Leonard Altobell whispered to me during the curtain calls, helped launch a long and not-too-shabby career.

CHAPTER EIGHT

Emma Jean Whittington

One of the plays that was mounted at the Rochester Summer Theater was the 1932 drama "The Devil Passes," by Ben Levy. In it the Devil claims to be God and He offers people what they want most in the world. Some are happy to discover they are not as selfish as they thought, but those who are seduced by the Devil end up hurt. I played the part of The Devil, a role that allowed for loud and declamatory emoting.

During the curtain call, while acknowledging the applause from an appreciative audience, I heard a young mid-western-accented female voice shout.

"Carl Reiner, I love you, I just love you and the way you played your part!"

The voice was coming from a comely young lady who was standing below the stage and waving her program at me.

"I'm Emma Jean Whittington," she shouted, "and I'm one of the new apprentices—can I please come backstage and speak with you— please!?"

After exchanging hellos, Emma Jean threw her arms around me, kissed my cheeks and continued heaping compliments on me and my performance.

By the end of that first week she had fallen deeply in love with me and told me so. I had fallen deeply 'in like' with her and willingly participated in the kissing and petting she had instituted in the open field behind our theater.

27

I was eighteen years old and had not gone 'all the way' with any of my former girlfriends. Emma Jean, on the other hand, told of wonderful but unsuccessful love affairs she had with two men. Her first was a steady boyfriend who was stolen away by her then best friend and the second with a man she loved but not deeply enough to marry.

She was very understanding of my situation and brought a blanket for us to lie on. For the possibility of some serious development arising, I had a condom tucked away in my wallet.

My second year as an actor was completely fulfilling. I played the leading roles in four productions—Macauley Connor in "The Philadelphia Story," Lloyd Lloyd in "Kiss the Boys Goodbye," Curley in "Of Mice and Men," Papa Bonaparte in "Golden Boy," and the arch villain in an old fashioned 'Mellerdrama.'

For the twelve weeks we were together, Emma Jean and I were inseparable. I learned of the impressive Whittington Family Tree which dated back to 1354 and her English forebears, one of which was the Lord Mayor of London. It was thought that the classic tale, "Dick Whittington's Cat" was written about this Mayor's cat.

When I caught a flu bug and was bedridden for two days, Emma Jean lovingly tended to me by bringing and feeding me hot soups and cereals.

At that time I was an opera buff and told Emma Jean, who knew nothing about opera, all about my favorite arias and the great tenors that sung them. She had never heard Enrico Caruso sing and when I returned to New York, I promised to send recordings of his greatest arias.

When our summer ended, it was Emma Jean who suggested that before she returned to Oklahoma and I to the Bronx, we spend a night making love in a bed. To that end, she reserved a room at a Rochester hotel where I experienced another 'first'—actually two 'firsts.' I had never slept in a hotel and I had never made love in a bed.

There were also two things about Emma Jean that set her apart from all others in my life, male or female. She was the only person I knew who could pilot a plane and owned the plane she piloted.

Being a man of my word, as soon as I returned home I went to record stores, found, among a dozen others, used RCA Red Seal recordings of Enrico Caruso singing "E Lucevan Le Stelle" from "La Tosca" and "Vesti La Giubba," from "Pagliacci."

I packed them carefully and mailed them to her. I was happy to hear that none were damaged in transit and happier to hear her say, "I just loved hearing those wonderful, operatic songs sung by such wonderful singers."

Soon after returning home from Avon, I auditioned for and was hired to tour with "The Avon Shakespearean Company."

I felt it a good omen that two theater companies that employed me had the word "Avon" connected to them.

CHAPTER NINE

Room and Board and The Bard

Soon after my summer sojourn in upstate New York, I found myself on a train traveling to Atlanta, Georgia to join the Avon Shakespeare Touring Company, whose actors were to be billeted at a downtown hotel. For the eight week tour, I was to be paid thirty dollars a week, the largest salary I had ever earned. I wrote Emma Jean about my lucky break and she became excited about the possibility of flying down to visit me.

A most heartening aspect of this job, besides the salary, was the opportunity to appear in an indoor theater. No longer would I have to act while moths and gnats fluttered about my head, and once, actually, into one of my fellow actor's mouth.

I had known about the south's Jim Crow laws, but had never before seen signs posted on toilet doors and drinking fountains that read, "For Whites Only," and "For Coloreds Only."

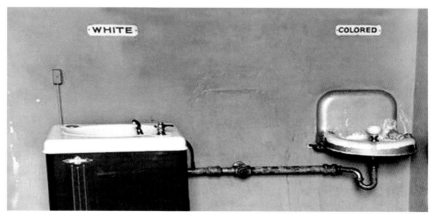

I was truly unnerved at seeing these signs blatantly expressing racial bigotry.

I was in for another unnerving moment, when I stepped on the shabby lobby tiles of the even shabbier "Hotel Tallulah." After checking in at the desk, I made my way up the stairs and met a kimono-clad young lady who smiled and asked me if I was lonely.

I smiled and naively explained, "I haven't been away from home that long."

That afternoon, after leaving the hotel and starting down the street to look for a coffee shop, I felt a powerful hand slip into my back pocket, twist it and actually lift me off the ground.

"Don't make me use my club!" a southern accented voice warned.

It was a cop doing his duty—arresting men who had solicited sex. He had assumed that if I exited the "Tallulah," that's what I had done. Using my best stage diction, I explained that I was a member of the "Avon Shakespearean Company" and would be staying at the hotel before going on tour. He glared at me, mumbled something, then walked away. I was unaware that the hotel's new management was in the process of evicting the prostitutes who, for many years, had rented rooms at the Tallulah to entertain their 'Gentlemen Callers.'

At the rehearsals which were held in the Hotel's ballroom, I learned from Harold Selman, the theater's co-owner and director, that, for two weeks before going on tour, we would rehearse three of our four plays.

Harold Selman had, earlier in his life, been a member of an esteemed theater company. He had once toured the continent playing roles in "Hamlet," "As You Like It," "The Comedy Of Errors" and "The Taming Of The Shrew," and now he was preparing to direct them.

We were scheduled to travel to southern colleges and high schools where, each afternoon, we would be performing one of the plays.

To ascertain how proficient each actor was in mouthing Shakespeare's words, the stage manager asked each of us to step up to the podium.

Lucky me, I was the first called. So that we would be standing eye-to-eye, Mr. Selman, a short, thin, wizened old man, stood on a small riser and pointed a quivering forefinger at me. In a beautifully sonorous tone, he lisped,

"Thay after me—'Now ith the winter of our dithcontent, may gloriouth thummer by the thon of York...' Then, with his a boney forefinger, Mr. Selman tapped the top of my head and lisped, "Thay!"

Mimicking his speech perfectly, I said, "Now ith the winter of our dithcontent may glorious thummer by the thon of York..." Mr. Selman stared at me for a moment, then tapped my head again and said, "Very good."

Feeling pleased with myself, I smiled as I returned to my seat. Gene Lyons, a fellow actor, asked, "What did you just do?"

"Exactly what he asked me to do... I impersonated him and said the lines like he did."

"Did he ask you to impersonate his stroke?"

"A stroke! Oh shit! I thought he lisped for effect, like in 'King John,' who had some sort of impediment."

In spite of my goof, I was cast for two leading roles, Orlando in "As You Like It," and Antipholus of Ephesus in "The Comedy of Errors," as well as King Claudius in "Hamlet," a smaller but substantial role. In "The Taming of The Shrew," I played two small parts, Lucentio and The Tailor.

We worked long hours rehearsing "As You Like It," "The Comedy of Errors" and "The Taming of The Shrew," the plays we would be doing during the first seven weeks of our tour. "Hamlet" was not scheduled to be performed until our last week.

During rehearsals of "As You Like It," I found the actress who played Orlando's love interest, Rosalind, to be most attractive. Her name was Helene and even though I was still committed to Emma Jean, I was tempted to learn more about this blonde haired vision with the smashing figure.

During our first rehearsal of the scene in "As You Like It" where Rosalind pours out her heart to Orlando, all lustful thoughts I had of Helene vanished. What did it was listening to Helene's monotonous and boring delivery of Shakespeare's words. For the rest of the tour Helene butchered the Bard's beautiful prose, but I managed to find a way to look at her adoringly.

As much as I shuddered every time I had to play Orlando, I happily looked forward to playing Antipholus of Ephesus in "The Comedy Of Errors." Not only was the play a crowd pleaser, but Gene Lyons, the actor who played my twin brother, Antipholus of Syracuse, was a good actor who soon became a good buddy. We managed to appear like identical twins, even though I was dark haired, three inches taller than Gene and had sturdy legs, while Gene had blond hair and thin legs. What helped was both of us donning blond wigs, my slouching whenever we stood side by side and Gene, to buff up his calf muscles, stuffed symmetrical pads into his tights.

I can still get a smile when I relate a compliment I once overheard after a performance at a high school in Decatur, Georgia. A young girl with a delightful down-home accent asked our stage manager,

"Suh, ah wonder ifn ah cn git 'Ansyphillis' aunagraph?"

"Which Ansyphillis' autograph do you want?" he kidded, "Ephesus or Syracuse?"

She thought for a moment before replying, "The wun with the purty legs!"

Gene and I became lifelong friends and his legs and personality were good enough to snare a delightful young actress, Peggy Kovac, who, on our tour, became his girlfriend and, not long after returning to New York, his wife.

Besides acting, Mr. Selman had assigned other roles for Gene and me to fill–roles that were integral in keeping our company running smoothly.

Gene and I were, also, in charge of the wardrobe. We would pack and unpack a trunk that held the sweaty, foul odored costumes our actors had worn that day. These classic vestments had once been worn by E. H. Southern and Julia Marlowe, the stars of the once famous "Southern and Marlow Shakespearean Touring Company."

They were fashioned of heavy woolen velour and brocaded silks that had not been washed or dry cleaned in decades. Each time Gene and I would set the trunk down in an open field we would hold our breath, throw open the trunk's lid and dash away—not to return until the foul odors had wafted off.

Then to sun dry them, we hung them on a clothes line that we had rigged in an open field. After an hour, the actors would claim their damp, slightly less smelly costumes, don them for that day's performance and add fresh perspiration.

After the tour ended, Gene and Peggy Lyons went back to New York and rented a small apartment in the Luxor Hotel on West 46th Street which has since been razed. That apartment became my weigh station whenever I came to Manhattan to look for work. Five days a week I traveled from my parents' home in the Bronx to haunt the offices of Broadway's theatrical agents and producers.

Eons later, when producing "The Dick Van Dyke Show," I had the opportunity to cast Gene Lyons to play Ray Murdock, a deep probing, incendiary Mike Wallace-type host who...

...with mean skewered questions made good and kind Dick Van Dyke sweat & squirm.

Gene went on to have a successful career in films and television, and at one time was lucky enough to date Grace Kelly.

CHAPTER TEN

Oh Gertrude, Oh Claudius

On our way to Opelika, Alabama to perform "Kiss Me Kate," the one play that allowed me to recharge my battery, we received a most disquieting piece of news. The head of the Drama department at Opelika's college brought to our stage manager's attention that since they had recently mounted their own version of "Kiss Me Kate," they preferred we perform "Hamlet."

As King Claudius, I was clad in woolen tights and a gold trimmed black velvet cape... a costume that looked a lot better than it smelled.

When it came time to deliver my lines, I managed all his words, starting with: "How is it Hamlet that the clouds still hang on thee?"

Having been told that we would not be performing Hamlet for three weeks, I had not yet learned my lines.

I carried my script with me and tried to learn my lines while riding in the back of the station wagon, or airing out the smelly wardrobe or when lying in bed at night. I went over and over Claudius' lines until those few dozen lines had been lightly committed to memory. I envisioned them sitting precariously atop my brain and feared that tilting my head would cause Claudius' words to slip out my ear.

After one or two more exchanges, I started to deliver the speech that I worried would slip out of my ear. I declaimed, "Oh Gertrude, Gertrude, when sorrows come they come not in single files but in battalions... the poor people muddied in their thoughts of poor Polonious' death do... do..."

Here my mind went completely blank and I knew that Gene Lyons, playing Laertes, was waiting in the wings to hear his cue to enter... a cue that I never gave him. What I gave him was a garbled gibberish speech I had once heard the double talk artist, Cliff Nazarro, spout. Using my best Shakespearean elocution, I emoted:

"When Portisan and Uncle Snazzy, lilt the passing Chahaqua tis time to wend Lipesnard and greener fields of framital. So sassafrass the buttersnay and whipsnatch every rondenal– 'tis time to splay, 'tis time to stow but please, cliff me not the nazzaro!"

I continued to invent classic sounding gobbledygook while Gene Lyons remained in the wings, waiting to hear his cue to come onstage. As my panic level rose, the pitch and volume of my speech kept getting higher and louder, as I declaimed:

"That thou in the nyphous orizons doth dare to mock the very fortistan of cumolous, frangile and punditoruousness of thy sanctured and drillions of copitons, do dare to actify and thereboy doth cause to slash and fulminate the very calls of Framital, Hecuba, Rubitus and all thy unvirtuous calor, slake and vicissitudionous shall clems for an eternity! Fie, fie on thee and thy boodendas and frolicking freakitudinous flatmongers, who do portent my grief and my stricken plounds."

For a good five or six minutes, with my fists pumping and my voice screaming unintelligibly, I railed and railed, hoping that Laertes would come on stage and save me. He never did, but to my amazement, the audience did. They gave me a round of solid applause. Some students actually stood up and requested an encore, which I was not about to give them. I had never been more embarrassed.

It was not till days later, when Gene described to people who had not been in the theater, the triumphant performance I had given and asked that I give them a sample of the gibberish, did I realize that I might very well have a new, useful tool in my acting arsenal. Little did I know that years later I would use it on "Your Show Of Shows" in exchanges with Sid Caesar who, hands down, was the greatest double talk artist in history.

I finally did manage to learn Claudius' speech and the next time we played Hamlet I delivered it flawlessly and received sparse applause. I concluded that Shakespeare's words were nowhere near as entertaining and effective as mine.

While on tour, Emma Jean Whittington and I had been corresponding regularly and it was in Opelika, Alabama, that I received a call from her. She asked how I felt about her flying to Opelika for a quick visit, and I told her that we would have very little time together as our troupe never spent more than a night in each town. Emma was a lovely girl and a good person, but I had begun to feel that our relationship might be coming to an end. We had little in common and it soon became clear to both of us that we were not meant for each other.

Ahh, c'est la darn vie.

CHAPTER ELEVEN

NYA Is Not Nya Nya but Yeah Yeah!

After my Shakespearean tour and an eighty dollars a week salary, I returned to New York and secured a job in radio which paid twenty-two dollars and fifty cents per month. It was 1940, and once again it was our President and caring government leaders who stepped up and instituted "The NYA, 'The National Youth Administration,'" whose function was to fund programs that would employ writers, actors, directors and musicians.

The NYA studios were housed on the seventh floor of a thirteen storied building located at 1697 Broadway between 53rd and 54th streets.

On the ground floor of this terra cotta structure was a large theater,

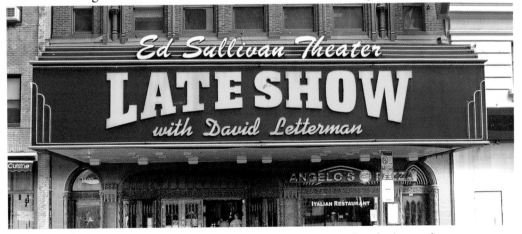

which would one day become "The Ed Sullivan Theater" and telecast shows.

The NYA workshop consisted of two rooms, one being a large room where actors and musicians rehearsed and broadcast their shows. The second room was a glass-enclosed control booth from which engineers would send out our shows to appreciative audiences. I use the word appreciative advisedly because some of our radio plays were written by the celebrated author Norman Corwin.

His dramas were initially broadcast on the CBS network. Mr. Corwin had offered these scripts free of charge and it was an offer our director Larry Menkin was happy to accept.

I recall fondly a Norman Corwin radio play, "My Client Curly," in which I had the opportunity to play the manager of a 'Song & Dance' caterpillar named "Curly." In 1944, a film version was made of "My Client Curly," re-titled, "Once Upon a Time." For the part of Curley's manager, the studio hired not me but Cary Grant.

Another series we did at the workshop was a futuristic one whose title escapes me. All the actors auditioned to play the program's narrator, and thanks to the classic accent I had honed on my recent Shakespearean tour, I was given the role.

To achieve an eerie, echo-like effect, our director had opened the lid of a grand piano, placed a microphone on its strings then bade me to put my head in the piano.

Then he cued me to say my lines which were,

"My voice as ageless as the moon and sun and stars echoes endlessly through the corridors of centuries."

By mustering my deepest stentorian voice, and speaking in a declamatory, legato rhythm, it sounded like this:

"MMMMYYYYYYYYYY VOOOOOOOOOOIIIIIIIIICE AS AAAAGELESSSSSS AS THE MOOOOOOOON AND SUUUUUUUNNNNN AND STAAAAARS ECCHHOOOOES ENNNNNDDDDDLESSSSLLLYY THROUUUUUUGH THE COOORRRRRIDOOOOORS OF CEEEENNNNTUUURIEEEEEEEEEEEEEEEEEEES!"

41

After our southern tour and having made a lifelong friend of Gene Lyons, I made a similar relationship with Howard Morris, a fellow NYA employee. Howard, a height-challenged actor, was the best educated and versatile member of our group, had a wonderful speaking voice and the ability to correctly pronounce the names of classical composers and their compositions. Auditions were held for someone to announce the following lines:

"The NYA Youth Symphony will now perform for you, 'Eine Kleine Nachtmusik, Serenade number 13 for Strings in G Major by Wolfgang Amadeus Mozart.'"

Howard Morris was given the job because he pronounced the composer's name "M o t e-s a r t," as it was meant to be pronounced, and not "M o z z a r t," as the rest of us did.

One late afternoon, while on a bus going home from work, Howard, who was 3 years older than I, told me of receiving his Army draft notice. Being short and weighing a hundred twenty-nine pounds, three below the required weight, I assured him that he'd be rejected and back at work the next day.

The following day Howard told me that, after a sleepless night, he had eaten breakfast and, to calm himself before going to the draft board, had drunk a couple glasses of water. The breakfast and the liquids he gulped down, plus not having gone to the toilet, ballooned him to the proscribed weight. Thus, Howie, as I came to call him, was inducted into the U.S. Armed Forces.

After our meeting on that fateful day in 1940, Howie and I did not meet again until 1943 when, in Hawaii, he helped me to become a member of the U.S. Army's Entertainment Section.

CHAPTER TWELVE

The Merry Widow Made Me A Union Member

It was January 1940 and on March 20th of that year I would turn eighteen and could then expect to receive my draft notice. When in the Army, I was anxious to be assigned to Special Services where I could continue to perform and entertain. I figured that my chances might be enhanced were I a member of Actor's Equity, a theatrical union. The only way I could get a union card was to get a job in a Broadway play and to that end, I bought a copy of "Weekly Variety," and scoured its pages. The only jobs being offered were for chorus singers to join a traveling production of Franz Lehar's "The Merry Widow."

At the audition, when asked about my draft status, I told them it would be months before I would be called—an untruth but I was desperate to get a Union card.

I passed the audition and was assigned to play one of the six soldiers in the chorus who guard The Merry Widow, who hails from the mythical nation of Moldavia. The Widow was portrayed by Muriel Angelus, a beautiful and talented lyric soprano.

The role of her lover, Count Danilo, was played by a tenor who, if still alive, will be happy I cannot recall his name.

At every performance, my chorus buddy, Charles Dubin, and I would wager a quarter that the tenor who played Count Danilo would, when singing "Ladies Choice," muff the high C at the end of the song. Lucky for the audience, most times he hit it.

I did enjoy my job, for besides getting to sing:

"I'm off to Chez Maxine
Where pleasure is the thing,
With music, wine and dancing,
Add pleasure to romancing."

We also got to give voice to:

"Ladies choice, let this manly heart rejoice,
"Let me be the only one
Who finds the radiance of the sun..."

(That's all the lyrics I recall... frchrissakes it's 75 years ago)

Charles Dubin and I, as members of the chorus, managed to inject a piece of business that got a big laugh from the audience. Our little shtick came after we two soldiers marched on stage and after saluting the Merry Widow we saluted each other. As we stood nose to nose, we touched our hands to our brows, then lowered them, saluted each other from our belt buckles and finished off with a snappy patty cake before putting a fingertip up our noses.

Years after World War II ended, Charlie Dubin and I happened to meet on Broadway and without saying a word, we greeted each other with the authentic and patented Moldavian salute!

During the ugly repressive McCarthy era, Charles was blacklisted twice, first in 1952, then in 1958. At  that time, he appeared before the House Committee on Un-American Activities, explained that he was not a Communist Party member, had never known anyone in the party nor of any activity contrary to the interests of the United States, but also believed in his right not to testify. Charles' career as a daring director in television's early years stalled after he refused to answer those questions. However in 1963, Charles got a big break when writer/producer Larry Gelbart hired Charles to direct an hour-long Judy Garland special... which was nominated for an Emmy.

Charles never looked back after those dark days and went on to have a successful and satisfying career as a television director. He directed forty-four episodes of "M*A*S*H," more than anyone else.

Charles Dubin   Mike Farrell   Alan Alda   David Ogden Stiers   Loretta Swit

45

CHAPTER THIRTEEN

Camping It Up At Camp Crowder Missouri

In 1943 at Camp Crowder, a patient Signal Corps instructor decided that I had the potential to learn how to use a telegrapher's key to send Morse coded messages over a wire.

I am proud to say in a few weeks I mastered the code and was able to send, receive and decipher the series of dots and dashes that translated into words—words that would hopefully lead to military victories that could end the war.

Without consulting Google, I will attempt to determine how many letters of the alphabet I can still put into Mr. Morse's dots and dashes.

   a   b   c   d   e   f

Just checked Google and except for the 'e,' I was a total failure.

FYI: The correct codes for those letters are:

   a   b   c   d   e   f

If ever I need help, I do remember that the code for SOS is:

Camp Crowder, besides affording me the opportunity to learn Morse Code, gave me a platform to display my wares as an entertainer. One or two nights a week, on the stage of our company's Recreation Hall, I received a goodly amount of applause, laughs and approbation for telling jokes and doing fairly good impressions of film stars.

It was at Company Eight's Recreation Hall that I met Louis Neistadt, a young comedian who was the 'Rec' Hall's resident M. C.

I am not sure how it started but, on that stage, after performing my act, I started to interview Louis. I asked him the kind of questions that, twenty five years later, I would be posing to Mel Brooks'"2000 Year Old Man."

At one point I asked Corporal Neistadt to discuss the items that go into the full field pack that combat soldiers were required to carry. I don't remember most of the items he packed but I'll never forget the items that got the biggest laughs.

When I asked about sending and receiving mail from loved ones, he informed me that there are no mail boxes in the jungle, and if you wanted to contact your loved ones, you'd write a note on a small piece of paper, fold it and slip it into the tiny pouch strapped to the leg of the carrier pigeon you carry in your full field pack. When I questioned him about the efficacy of packing a live pigeon, he ignored me and continued,

"And do not, I repeat, DO NOT forget to pack a Coca Cola bottle top!"

When asked, "Why would I need a bottle top?"

"It's not for you," Louis replied, "it's the carrier pigeon's latrine."

Very soon after playing straight man for Louis, my outfit was shipped out of Camp Crowder and it was many moons before we met again in New York City. I was thrilled to be present when Cpl. Louis Neistadt morphed from my funny army buddy into a funny co-starring actor in the Broadway musical "Inside USA," which starred Bea Lillie...

...and Jack Haley, whose role I understudied. For your entertainment, here are the lyrics to the song I never got to perform, "Little Old Rhode Island."

Old whiskey comes from old Kentucky
Ain't the country lucky
New Jersey gives us glue
And you, you come from Rhode Island
And little old Rhode Island is famous for you
Grand canyons come from Colorado
Gold comes from Nevada
Divorces also do
And you, you come from Rhode Island
Little old Rhode Island is famous for you
Pencils come from Pennsylvania
Vests from Vest Virginia
And Tents from Tennessee
They know mink where they grow in Wyo mink
A camp chair in New Hampshire, that's for me
And minnows come from Minnesota
Coats come from Dakota
But why should you be blue
For you, you come from Rhode Island
Don't let them ride Rhode Island
It's famous for you

I was present when our producer Arthur Schwartz convinced Louis Neistadt that changing his hard-to-pronounce name to Louis Nye would help him further his career. In the next 40 years on TV, in night clubs and film, Louis Neistadt and Louis Nye made quite a name for themselves.

Louis Nye as bon-vivant Gordon Hathaway on The Steve Allen Show.

48

CHAPTER FOURTEEN

Georgetown Is My Kind Of Town

At one point in my army career, I was sent to Laramie, Wyoming to be evaluated for reassignment. Upon learning that I had studied French at Evander Childs High School, the powers that be ordered me to pack my bags for the trip to Washington, D. C. where, at the University of Georgetown's School of Foreign Services, I would start a program that would train me to become a French interpreter.

It was at the end of my eleven month stay at the University that I experienced the most triumphant day of my budding career in comedy.

The year was 1942 and it was a week before Christmas, when our commanding officer, Captain Dixon, called me into his office.

During my stay at the University, Captain Dixon, who had seen me perform as a Master of Ceremonies at a local USO, asked if I would produce a Christmas Day variety show to present at Gaston Hall. I was thrilled to be asked and immediately went to work. I cobbled together a show that included three or four talented soldiers in our unit, a guitarist-singer, Eddie Riley, who sang a show stopping rendition of "Paper Doll," a baritone, Howard Hartman, who belted out operatic arias, and four soldiers who sang old standards in close-harmony. Their names escape me, but they were gooooood.

That would be our Christmas extravaganza, three acts and myself as emcee-monologist.

As part of my act, I planned to do my impressions of motion picture stars but, as show day drew near, I decided that instead of doing my standby impersonations, it might be more fun if I did impressions of our Jesuit teachers and instructors.

I was able to mimic Father Verhoosel, a hip Jesuit Priest who had a thick Belgian accent and spoke in a deep monotone. It was difficult to understand what he was saying but his sonorous, room-filling voice was comforting.

I was able to do a spot-on impression of Professor Coutinho, a Portuguese professor who we were told helped to create Portugal's Falangist government. Professor Coutinho was a political scientist who, early in his career, was a good friend of a Marxist and one of the architects of the Russian revolution, Vladimir Lenin.

Many of our students leaned to the left and when they heard that Professor Coutinho knew Lenin personally, they could not wait to hear what the famous revolutionary was like. Their first question was,

"What was Lenin like?"

Professor Coutinho, with his high-pitched voice, in short, staccato, Portuguese accented sentences, did not tell us what Lenin was like, but rather, what he liked to eat. The Professor spoke of their meeting at a Paris bistro and described, in great detail, the "Little Chocolate Nougats" that Lenin ordered every day. Professor Coutinho, not certain we knew what a Chocolate Nougat was, took a great deal of time to describe precisely what a Nougat looked like and tasted like. He excitedly inumerated all the chocolate ingredients that were laced through it.

After hearing more than we needed to know about Chocolate Nougats and Lenin's love of them, one of our group interrupted the Professor and asked if he might tell us more about "Lenin the man."

"Lenin was nice man, very nice man," the Professor happily replied. I call him Vladimir... Vladimir little taller than me—had small hands—he very smart man, very, very smart man—had good ideas—many good ideas—also short, pointy beard—from photograph you see what kind beard."

I was thoroughly convinced that Lenin was smart, a very nice man, had a pointy beard, loved and knew everything there was to know about Chocolate Nougats.

By show time, seated in Georgetown University's staid Gaston Hall were the three hundred soldiers from our Company E, a few dozen Priests, professors and teachers and a scattering of state department officials—all primed to enjoy our Christmas offering.

Generally, performers are nervous before walking out onto a stage, but this night, because I was also the producer, it was not nervousness I was feeling but rather, a numbed excitement. I knew that the acts I had gathered would do well, but I had no clue as to how the powers-that-be would react to material I had never before performed.

Would they, who control my fate, smile and find me funny or would they frown and find me a perfect candidate for a court martial?

Just as I had foreseen, all the performers on the bill did great. I was particularly heartened by the cries for encores that each of our musical acts received. My army buddies were very supportive and laughed loudly when I did my impressions of our professors, and I was relieved to see that most faculty members were either laughing or smiling. After delivering my impression of Professor Coutinho, I walked off to appreciative applause and did not return for a bow. Instead, I ran around to the back of the stage and, after the applause had petered out, I made an entrance, not as myself, but as someone whose gait and body language I hoped they would recognize, and they did. A hush fell over the auditorium, a hush that hid the collective thought, "Oh no, he's not going to do an impression of him!"

The 'him' they never dreamed I would have the guts to impersonate was the Dean of the School of Foreign Service, Reverend Father Edmund A. Walsh.

Once a week, all the University's students were present in this very hall when Father Walsh delivered a lecture on Geopolitics, a subject of which he was the preeminent scholar. Dean Walsh was a frequent visitor to the White House and State Department, where he was asked by top government and military officials for his opinion on the Geopolitical problems that were besetting Europe and the world.

General Douglas MacArthur & Father Walsh

At Gaston Hall, we often heard him expound on his "Theory of the Heartland."

"Whoever controls the Heartland," he insisted, "controls all of Europe, and therefore, all of the civilized world! That is why it is imperative that The United States use its military might to seize this territory before the Russians do!"

It did not concern him that the Russians and Americans were fighting side by side to rid the world of Hitler and Nazism. Under no circumstance could Father Walsh accept Godless Russia as his ally.

As one might expect, some outraged student fed Father Walsh's statements to the then liberal New York Post, whose headline the following day screamed,

"Government Sponsored Fascism at Georgetown!"

It naturally caused quite a brouhaha. Nonetheless, on that Christmas afternoon, I, approximating Father Walsh's mien, strode to the lectern and behaved as if I were looking at an audience who had respectfully greeted me by standing up. I nodded benignly and uttered a spot-on impersonation of Father Walsh's deep, well modulated voice, instructing the seated audience to:

"Please be seated!"

I was greeted by a gasp and a few guarded chuckles. The gasp was from those who were shocked that I would dare to make fun of our revered Dean. The guarded chuckles were from those who were aware that rows full of clergy and teachers were in the balcony looking down at them. To laugh at jokes that skewered Father Walsh would not be the most politic thing to do—and that's what we did, I skewered and they laughed!

Pitching my voice to Father Walsh's register and using his mellifluous tone and cadence, I launched into a version of his lecture on "The Heartland," ending with:

"While it may have been true that 'Whoever controls The Heartland controls all of Europe', there is a newer and truer truth emerging about 'The Heartland'! I have just this night been informed by a ranking member of our State Department that adjacent to 'The Heartland,' two new territories have been discovered. They are 'The Liverland' and the 'The Onionland'. On our blessed earth was there ever anything more compatible or gastronomically mated than Liver and Onions? A rapprochement between the Heart, Liver and Onion Land will, I daresay, bring everlasting happiness to our beloved Homeland."

You will have to take my word for it, but the laughs that this silly parody engendered were seismic, way beyond what it deserved. No doubt the austerity of Gaston Hall, the constituency of the audience and the suicidal nature of the undertaking was, in great measure, the reason for its success.

I spent the rest of that day accepting and enjoying the accolades I received from my buddies. At night, as I lay in my bunk, I took great pleasure recalling the images of Father Verhoosel, Professor Coutinho and the many men of cloth, seated in the balcony, pounding on the railing and laughing uncontrollably at my impression of Father Edmond J. Walsh. Had Father Walsh been present, I doubt they would have allowed themselves to act as they did.

I am, at this moment, reliving and, once again, enjoying this special day in my life.

Company "E"
Army Specialized Training
School of Foreign Service — Georgetown University
Washington D.C.   June 25, 1943

CHAPTER FIFTEEN

Sept. 2, 1945–VJ Day and CR Day

At one point, during the War, I was assigned to the 3117th Signal Battalion in Joplin, Missouri, where I was trained to be a teletype operator. Most of our days were spent learning to type at a proscribed number of words per minute and studying the manual's procedures for the proper sending and receiving of voice and teletyped messages.

Our group, after being certified as Message Center operators, boarded a ship and sailed on a non-pacific, Pacific Ocean. A roiling sea did not allow me to keep a single meal down during our long crossing on a Jerry-built Liberty Ship that was not equipped with stabilizers.

Finally, we docked in Oahu and, after having my first solid food in days, I learned that our group was assigned to a detachment and scheduled to be shipped to an unknown destination, that is, unknown to us. At this point, fate stepped in and changed the trajectory of my Army career and, I daresay, of my life. It was a poster that hung in our Recreation Room inviting service men to attend a performance of Hamlet that was being held at the University Of Hawaii. It was billed as the "G. I. Hamlet" and was being performed by soldiers of an entertainment section who wore their Army issued fatigue uniforms.

My best buddy Sol Pomerantz and I decided to spend our last night in Oahu soaking up culture. We knew that the play was worth attending as it starred, as Hamlet, the celebrated Broadway star, Maurice Evans, who was then a Major in the United States Army.

Major Evans and the cast were excellent and the happy surprise for me was the presence of Howard Morris, the actor who played Laertes. Howie was my old compatriot with whom I had worked at the NYA Radio Workshop. This oil portrait of Howie as Laertes was painted by Ray Olivere, who was then a member of the entertainment section and presently a world renowned portraitist.

Backstage I wanted to congratulate Howie on his performance but didn't get a word out before he asked, "Carl, do you have a comedy act?" Not aware then that my old acting buddy was now the sergeant in charge of recruiting talent for shows that performed at Army bases, I told him, "I do have an act." He then asked me if I would audition for Major Evans and his assistant, Captain Allen Ludden.

Yes, the Allen Ludden who, after the war, hosted TV's popular game show, "Password," where he met and married one of the contestants, Betty White.

I explained to Howie that I would like to audition but I was shipping out the following night. Sol suggested that even if I could not join their company, I should audition and find out how good I was.

"See what professionals think of your act," he counseled.

The following morning, I did my impression of Monty The Talking Dog doing his impressions of celebrities. Captain Ludden agreed that I would be a welcome addition to their troupe. I told them that I was shipping out the following day, but they obviously wanted me badly enough to convince General Richardson, the head of the Central Pacific Base Command, that I be transferred to the Entertainment Section.

As the comedy star of "Shape Ahoy," for which I wrote the sketches, we played at Army bases on islands throughout the Pacific. I was loudly applauded for my impression of Monty The Talking Dog doing his spot-on impressions of Jimmy Stewart, Charles Boyer, Akim Tamiroff and Ronald Colman.

One year later, on VJ Day, I miraculously found myself on Iwo Jima, standing on a jerry-built stage, entertaining the members of my old outfit, the 3117th Signal Battalion.

CHAPTER SIXTEEN

From One Good Audition I Acquire
One Fair Job & One Great Job

In 1946, after serving in the Army for three years, I found myself back in New York and auditioning for a summer job as the resident Emcee of the Lake Spofford Hotel in New Hamshire.

In a William Morris Agent's rehearsal room I auditioned for Abe Jacobson, the non-smiling owner of the Lake Spofford Hotel, by doing my impressions of movie stars. From his lack of response I was certain that Mr. Jacobson would not hire me. I was wrong, not only did he hire me, but he told me that I was "resilient," and promised that, with his coaching, I'd become "A big star!"

Unbeknownst to me, Herman Levin, a Broadway producer, had seen that audition but had not heard it. He was looking through the small rehearsal room window door and saw a tall, not too bad looking young man making comical faces, striking poses and being animated enough to assay the leading role in the touring company of "Call Me Mister."

The role on Broadway was played by the gifted comedian, Jules Munshin, who had taken the town by storm.

The show's producers were Herman Levin and Melvyn Douglas. Mr. Douglas, who left all of the mundane business dealings to Herman Levin, was a popular film actor who had been in many classic films, the most memorable being "Ninotchka," in which he co-starred with Greta Garbo.

Mr. Levin, who had signed Jules Munshin to a non-binding, short term contract for two hundred dollars a week, was roiled when his disgruntled star, who had gotten rave reviews, threatened to leave the show unless they doubled his original salary.

To avoid being faced again with this situation, Mr. Levin offered me a contract that contained a clause that, I daresay, had never before been written into any Equity contract. It stated that for the first two weeks I was to receive two hundred dollars a week and, if deemed worthy to continue playing the part, I would receive a fifty dollar raise. It further stipulated that I waived all rights to renegotiate my contract no matter how many rave reviews I received.

In spite of this weird contract, it was the happiest and most exciting time of my life! Not only had I secured a plum job, but I had the wherewithal to arrange for my dear wife Estelle to accompany me to Boston, where "Call Me Mister" was scheduled to open its national tour.

Our happiness quotient spiked when we learned that, during our stay at Lake Spofford Hotel, we had happily conceived what was to be our firstborn.

Each week in Boston our joy increased, as did the show's box office receipts and Estelle's belly. Our planned two week stay in Boston became a three month stay. To save money for what we would need to support our growing family, we checked out of the expensive room at the Bradford Roof Hotel and moved into a tiny, two room apartment that had been crudely constructed in the basement of a dilapidated one story house. At that time I stood six feet, one and a half inches tall and the ceiling of our new abode was a mere two inches higher.

One day my wife and I dared to invite a cast member who was six feet five inches tall and whose name escapes me.

After seeing him stoop over as he entered our living room, we immediately invited him to sit down at our small dining room table. The chairs could barely accommodate his frame and he had to sit side-saddle while he ate and enjoyed a remarkably delicious dinner Estelle had cooked on, what was essentially, a toy stove. I remember the three of us laughing at the "Gulliver's Travels" aspect of our low-ceilinged Lilliputian dinner party.

Before finishing our Boston run, Estelle flew to New York, where she gave birth to our son Robert.

Rob at six months.

On its way to Chicago, our show was booked for one week stands in Philadelphia, Pittsburgh, Detroit and Cleveland. "Call Me Mister" received rave reviews and I was thrilled to be singled out for my "sterling performance." I sent these reviews to my dear, supportive wife, who pasted them in the albums I am now using to tell this self-aggrandizing story.

For our upcoming stop at Chicago's Blackstone Theater, our producers planned to drop anchor for another three month run. The positive reviews we received in every town made for sold out theaters, and we were certain that nothing could derail us.

We had second thoughts when, traveling from Detroit to Chicago, a sniper, in the guise of a theater critic, wrote an article that our stage manager, Biff Liff, called to our attention. The sniper-critic was Claudia Cassidy, one of the most revered and powerful reviewers in the country. For "The Chicago Tribune," Ms. Cassidy wrote that she had seen the original production of "Call Me Mister" in New York and found it dull and boring. She recommended that to avoid embarrassment, we by-pass Chicago and go straight on to San Francisco.

On opening night, every member of the cast, eager to disprove Miss Cassidy's assessment, gave the best and most energetic performances our bodies could muster. At the end of the first act, we were heartened by huge applause, but quickly disheartened when Biff Liff, who was monitoring Ms. Cassidy's reactions, reported that as the curtain fell she bolted from her seat, left the theater... and did not return for the second act.

I remember waking up early, riffling though the newspaper and being prepared to wince at Ms. Cassidy's review. My wince turned into a grin when I learned that the reason she bolted from the theater was to make the deadline for the rave review she would write. She explained that she could not wait to return the following night and see the second act.

I checked my scrapbooks, hoping to find and include a copy of that second rave review, but struck out. Suffice it to say that had I been a politician, Ms. Cassidy's second review of my performance would have catapulted me to a nomination for President, but what it actually did was lengthen our run in Chicago from six weeks to six months.

CHAPTER SEVENTEEN

Keep Talking

After my days performing as Sid Caesar's second banana on "Your Show of Shows," an enterprising producer at CBS offered me the opportunity to host "Keep Talking," a new prime time game show.

The show involved a panel of talented celebrities who were divided into two teams. I would give each player a secret word to use in a story that they would have to ad-lib and the other team then had to guess what that secret word was. (I imagine it's obvious to you why the show had a short life.) Below is the toupeed host of "Keep Talking" and on the following pages are the clever, creative celebrities.

Elaine May   Peggy Cass   Vincent Price

Joey Bishop   Morey Amsterdam   Orson Bean

Danny Dayton   Paul Winchell   Audrey Meadows

Merv Griffin   Pat Carroll   Monty Hall

64

The Celebrity Game

In 1964-65, once again I was invited to act as the host of a new and original game show, appropriately entitled "The Celebrity Game." Its panel was composed of many of the most popular celebrities of the day.

"The Celebrity Game," a retooled version of Merrill Heatter and Bob Quigley's earlier "People Will Talk," had an elegant set and a formally-dressed nine-member celebrity panel and three competing contestants.

As the host, I posed moral-type questions to our panel of celebrities, questions such as, "Can most women keep a secret?" and "Should a man shave in a gas station restroom?" to which the celebrities secretly recorded either a "yes" or "no" vote. The three contestants locked in their vote as to how they believed the majority would answer. I then asked the celebrities for their answers and why they responded the way they did. Their responses were funny enough to keep the studio audience laughing and the sponsors happy.

On the following pages are seventy-seven stars that made multiple appearances on our weekly show. I credit our show with the fact that one of our celebrities made enough fans with his appearances that it vaunted him into a very high level, well-paying job. How many of you recognize that man who was flanked by Dorothy Lamour and Pearl Bailey?

Dorothy Lamour

Ronald Reagan

Pearl Bailey

Groucho Marx

Eden Marx

Paul Lynde

Gisele MacKenzie

Frankie Avalon

Shelley Winters

Jim Backus

Zsa Zsa Gabor

Dale Robertson

67

Steve Allen   Joan Crawford   Charles Ruggles

Betty Hutton   Douglas Fairbanks   Hedy Lamar

Edgar Bergen   Elaine Stewart   Edd Byrnes

Art Linkletter   Mel Brooks   Basil Rathbone

Cliff Arquette   Godfrey Cambridge   Tina Louise

Paul Ford   Jane Meadows   Robert Mitchum

Jack Jones   June Allyson   Raymond Massey

John Forsythe   Abby Dalton   Miyoshi Umeki

Roddy McDowall Barbara McNair Allan Sherman

Anne Baxter Bob Newhart Abby Lane

Cornel Wilde Cliff Robertson Dana Wynter

Joseph Cotten Nick Adams Fred Gwynne

Dwayne Hickman   Martha Raye   Eartha Kitt

Shari Lewis   Lola Albright   Vic Damone

Jan Murray   Jack Palance   Hedda Hooper

Bill Cosby   Nick Adams   Walter Brennan

Morey Amsterdam

Mickey Rooney

Agnes Moorehead

George Jessel

Julie Newmar

George Hamilton

Marilyn Maxwell

Gloria Swanson

Ann Sothern

Rory Calhoun

Stephen Boyd

Cara Williams

Lizabeth Scott   Ken Murray   Broderick Crawford

Donna Loren   George Gobel   Sterling Holloway

John McGiver   Tammy Grimes   Oscar Levant

One exchange I had with Oscar Levant was memorable.

I called his attention to the fact that Zsa Zsa Gabor had made a comment that caused the audience and crew to roar with laughter.

"Oscar," I asked, "how is it you're the only one in the theater not laughing?"

"I would have liked to but it's been so long since I laughed, I'm afraid dust will come out."

At the end of the run a new daytime show was being developed based on "The Celebrity Game" and I was asked to be its host. I declined, explaining that my training was as a night-time host. However, I was happy to appear on an episode of the show entitled:

"Hollywood Squares" was first hosted by Bert Parks, then by Peter Marshall and in its last years, Tom Bergeron. Its long successful run started in 1965 and ended in 2004.

Soon after guesting on my last game show my movie career started. I was cast in my first and only starring role in a feature film, "The Russians Are Coming! The Russians Are Coming!" It was directed by Norman Jewison, who assembled a stellar cast. The film became an international hit and was said to have eased the tensions between the United States and The Soviet Union.

Carl Reiner as Walt Whittaker

CHAPTER NINETEEN

Three Macho Cowards

The Place: San Francisco Airport
The Time: Sunday 11:00p.m., Summer of 1965

Eva Marie Saint, Brian Keith, Norman Jewison, and I had just arrived from Los Angeles, having spent the weekend with our families. We were on our way back to northern California where, for the past few weeks, we had been on location filming "**The Russians Are Coming, The Russians Are Coming.**" On preparing to board the small plane for the connecting flight to Fort Bragg, a trip we had made without incident several times during the twelve-week shooting schedule, we were informed that there was going to be a "change of equipment." It was unsettling to hear about problems with the "equipment"—and who decided to call a big thing like an airplane "equipment?"

Ordinarily, the "equipment" we flew on was a twin-engine Beechcraft, but it seemed that the Beechcraft and our regular pilot were both ailing and unavailable.

76

We were assured that the replacement pilot and plane, a single-engine Cessna, were quite capable of getting us safely to the Wilmot Airport in Eureka. The small plane could uncomfortably accommodate four passengers. The least uncomfortable seat was the one next to the pilot. We, being gallant "guys," insisted that the "doll," Eva Marie Saint, sit in the cockpit. Brian Keith and I sat on a bench-like middle seat, and Norman Jewison, the narrowest of us, volunteered to sit behind us on the little fold-down jump seat, under which I stowed a shoe box containing a present I had bought for my six-year-old son, Lucas—a pair of cowboy boots that needed to be exchanged for the right size and right color.

From a nervous passenger's point of view, it was a rotten night for flying, but our pilot did not seem at all concerned that it was drizzling and the wind socks on the landing strip were plump and flapping in the breeze and that a fog appeared to be rolling in. We macho guys made jaunty comments about enjoying the adventure of taking off and flying in bad weather, and I wondered if I was the only one who was lying. Probably. Brian Keith, a very fine actor, an excellent drinker, and a rock steady man's man, seemed to be his cool, confident self—as was Norman Jewison, a happy-go-lucky Canadian, inured to pain and freezing winters—and Eva Marie Saint, whose composure and strength are built into her name. All seemed totally at ease, which had a calming effect on me.

I was not happy to hear that the flying time in our single-engine Cessna would be a bit longer than with the Beechcraft. In spite of the wind and the rain, we were cleared for takeoff and our pilot—whose name I didn't hear, though it sounded like Poncho or Ponchus, so I thought of him as Pontius pilot—Pontius pushed the throttle forward, and we started down the bumpy runway. As the plane picked up speed, the windshield was splattered with giant raindrops. What was a light drizzle had suddenly turned into a heavy downpour. The single-engine plane shuddered as it took off and immediately started swaying drunkenly from side to side, bouncing and bumping as it struggled to climb higher. The cabin became eerily silent. The pilot was concentrating hard on steadying the vibrating plane, and none of us dared distract him with questions. *"If it keeps bouncing like this, might the wings fall off?"* is one I wanted to ask but held my tongue, as did my fellow passengers. After what seemed like hours, but in reality was about ten minutes, I found it necessary to break the silence.

"Uh, sir," I asked, mustering a matter-of-fact tone, "what was that string of red lights we just passed—at eye level? I don't remember seeing those red lights on any of our previous flights."

"Oh, they were there, but you were probably flying a couple of thousand feet above them."

"What are they?" all of us asked.

"Santa Rosa airport's warning lights," Pontius advised us calmly, "keeps low-flying planes from crashing into structures lower than five hundred feet."

"Why aren't we up a couple of thousand feet?" I asked.

"Been trying to, but the winds and rain are sort of holding us down," he said. "Might have to stay at this altitude all the way to Eureka. You do have to get there tonight, don't you?"

Brian, Norman, and I agreed that we did. I did with less enthusiasm.

"If you're nervous about the bumps and bounces," he said, "I could put her down."

Again, each of the macho men, not wanting to appear like spineless wimps, agreed that we push on.

"Hey, fellers, this is a little too bumpy-bouncy for me," Eva said calmly but firmly, "why don't we just land in Santa Rosa and rent a car?"

Without a moment's hesitation, we all spoke up. "Fine with me, Eva." "If that's what you want." "If you're uncomfortable . . ."

On hearing our response, the pilot banked the plane sharply, made a U-turn and nosed the "equipment" toward the Santa Rosa airport. None of us were prepared for that kamikaze maneuver, and we found ourselves suddenly lying on our right sides. Accompanying the passengers' grunts and groans were the frightening sounds of a door flying open, a sudden rush of air, and a whooshing noise. It sounded as though something slid along the floor and bumped against the flapping door. The most disturbing sound of all was the "*Oh shit!*" that escaped from Norman Jewison a split second after hearing the sliding whooshing sound. All this activity happened directly behind my seat. Trying to be heard above the sound of the motor and the rushing air, I screamed, "*Norman are you all right?*" Getting no response, I twisted my head and body around as far as my seat belt would allow and saw—no Norman! I heard the sound of a small cargo door flapping against the fuselage, as I reached behind me and swung my arm back and forth, trying to touch Norman, all the while, screaming, "*Norman, are you there? Say something!*"

I will not vouch for the accuracy of all the dialogue in this scene, but I do remember announcing these words to my terrified friends: "I think we lost Norman!" I had good reason to believe that Norman had slid out of the plane, because all of the evidence supported this—the sliding, whooshing sound, the open cargo door flapping against the fuselage, and his not answering when I screamed his name. I continued to call his name as I loosened my belt and got into a position to see what the hell had happened—and what I saw sent a chill through me. Norman was not in the jump seat—the seat had sprung back up. My fear that Norman had fallen out of the plane was half-justified. Half of Norman was hanging outside the plane face-down and his bottom half was stretched out on the floor. His right hand was reaching for and vainly grabbing at the handle of the swinging cargo door. I held onto his belt as he continued being assaulted by a driving rain, a gale force wind, and the wash from the propeller. The elements were doing all they could to frustrate him, but our dogged, rain-soaked director, leaning out dangerously far, finally managed to catch the door handle. With minimum help from me, he shimmied his way back into the plane and pulled the door shut. He grimaced, and said, "Lost your kid's boots, sorry."

When the pilot had made his unannounced, fighter-pilot maneuver, the rubber bands that had been securing the cargo door snapped, the door flew open, and the sliding-whooshing sound I thought was Norman going to his death was made by the box of boots sliding along the floor and out the door.

I told Norman Jewison then, and many times since, that I would rather have lost fifty pairs of boots than have lost the indispensable services of the director of *The Russians Are Coming, The Russians Are Coming.* It was the one and only movie for which I received top billing.

After living through Norman Jewison's out-of-plane, out-of-body experience, we all endured another eight hours of terror being chauffeured to Fort Bragg by Brian Keith, one of the Macho Men, who never figured out which knobs controlled the radio, the air-conditioner, the horn, or the defogger. He steered the rented Buick in a heavy downpour, through cotton-candy fog, over tortuous mountain roads. To avoid veering off a cliff, he drove at six miles an hour while straddling the white line in the center of the two-lane road. I stared intently at that white line for most of the trip, and when we finally arrived at our motel, I felt like a hypnotized chicken. All of us were tired, grungy, and bedraggled. We had arrived on time and ready to shoot—but the company hadn't. The insistent rain had made it impossible to shoot the scheduled exterior scenes that day or the next or the next. We had risked our lives for nothing!

Recalling the day of our traumatic plane and car rides and our arrival at Fort Bragg triggered a memory of an extraordinary gathering that took place in my motel suite on a dark, rainy afternoon.

Present in the cramped living room of my motel suite were many of the film's actors, among them, Jonathan Winters, Alan Arkin, Theodore Bikel, Michael J. Pollard, Paul Ford, Cliff Norton, Richard Schall, and three of the Cessna Four, Eva Marie Saint, Brian Keith and myself.

Jonathan Winters   Alan Arkin   Theodore Bikel

Michael J. Pollard   Paul Ford   Cliff Norton   Richard Schall

Norman Jewison was off somewhere cursing and worrying, the only thing a director can do when horrible weather screws up his shooting schedule. Hearing complaints about how little there is to do on rainy days in a small, quaint town whose one movie theater is only open at night, I thought it would be nice to invite the bored cast members to my room to discuss antidotes to boredom, nibble Cheetos or whatever else room service could provide, and perhaps, play a game or two.

When someone said, "How about we play charades?" someone countered with "How about fuck charades?" and everyone agreed it was a lousy idea, including me, who suggested it.

I don't know what possessed me to suggest another game, but I did.

"Hey," I announced, "I know a game we can play that I bet you haven't played for a long time. I think it's the kind of game that, if we play seriously, could be very exciting and something we'll all remember fondly."

Here now is how I introduced the playing of "Ring Around The Rosy" to the cast of *The Russians Are Coming, the Russians Are Coming.*

"All right, gang," I said, "raise your hands if you don't know how to play "Ring Around The Rosy."

Some raised their hands, some raised their eyebrows, some laughed, and some did all three.

"When was the last time any of you played a really serious game of "Ring Around The Rosy?" was my next question.

All admitted that they had not played it since they were children, and some recalled playing it with their own children.

"But you have never played it with adults," I pointed out, "and I guarantee that if you do, you will find it a hundred times more satisfying than it ever was. So do I have any players for a serious game of "Ring Around The Rosy?"

And what a gemütlich group they were! I believe Eva Marie Saint and Theodore Bikel were the first to volunteer and were closely followed by Alan Arkin, Cliff Norton, Jonathan Winters, et al. To make room for our game, I moved all the chairs and tables aside and, without being instructed, all the players joined hands and formed an almost perfect circle. I believe one or two of them laughed. I was upset by their attitude, but I chose not to admonish them at that time. I stepped between two of those gigglers, took their hands and joined the group.

"Now, does anyone not know the lyrics to the song?" Jonathan Winters was sure he remembered them all but had a question.

"After 'Ashes, ashes' some little kids sang 'aw faw dow' instead of 'all fall down.' Which is preferred?"

"Either is acceptable, but I think the latter, 'all fall down' suits our group better. Okay, gang," I said, masking my excitement, "we'll do a practice round, at half speed, and we will circle to the right!"

"It's not going to be easy to fall down at half speed," Alan Arkin advised. "Should we just indicate falling down?"

"Right, Alan," I agreed, "we don't fall on this rehearsal. Ready? Ring around the . . ."

We had barely sung the first line when someone, I think it was Alan Arkin, started to laugh.

"Hold it, hold it!" I said, controlling my anger. "I didn't think I had to spell it out, but for the game to be fun, we have to play it seriously. If you don't think you can be serious, then you can all leave and we'll forget about it. Is that what you want? I think you'll be missing out on something special. What'll it be?"

Reluctantly, they all agreed to give it a go. "Very well, we are understood," I said, hopefully, "let's try again. Ring... around... the... rohh-sy... a pocket full of pohh-sy..."

The group went through the mock rehearsal and waited for my critique. "Well, well," I said, feigning disappointment, "that first attempt at playing the game was shoddy, which is what I anticipated, but what I find unforgivable is that half of the actors, who think of themselves as disciplined professionals, either suppressed giggles or laughed openly—and this, after I warned you of the consequences. I guess playing a serious game of ring around the rosy with you people is just not possible. Why don't you go back to your suites and bore yourselves to sleep."

I started to open the motel door, but turned back to deliver my parting thrust, which I delivered sincerely and with passion. "In case some of you have forgotten the origin of this song, let me refresh your memory. In the fifteenth century, the bubonic plague decimated half the population in the world and this charming little ditty, which was sung and performed by innocent English school children, described what happened to a victim after being infected with the plague. Little red spots would appear on the skin—ring around the rosy—followed by death and flowers—pocket full of posies—and finally, the cremation of the ashen-faced corpse—ashes, ashes, all fall down! I guess," I sighed resignedly, "you have all forgotten why it should be sung and played seriously, but if you can't be serious..."

"We can, we can!" "We'll be serious!" "Give us another chance!"

I will never forget being a part of these dedicated mature actors circling about as we sang a sober and dignified rendition of "Ring Around The Rosy." We sang it not once but four times, circling first to the right then to the left then falling down. The final rendition was the most difficult because by that time none of us could hold back the laughter that started building when we first agreed to be serious about acting silly.

CHAPTER TWENTY

Donald J. Trump

Fifty years later, on June 15th, 2015, when Donald Trump announced that he was running for President, I tweeted the first of my many heartfelt anti-Trump tweets:

carl reiner @carlreiner
The garbage spewed by the badly-bleached-blond-bouffant-buffoon belongs in the dumpster along with the Trumpster

     83   557

This is my 32nd tweet that hopefully enlightened the public to the real Mr. Trump. I am aware that many like-minded citizens have tweeted similar or better versions of Donald with a Pinocchio nose.

Since tweeting that, Donald Trump has become our 45th President and last night I dreamed that he proved it was a rigged election and proclaimed himself King Donald The First.

Oceans 11:45 PM

One of the exciting things about being in show business is that, at any time, and usually when you are least expecting it, something will drop from nowhere, and offer a challenge that you'd be a fool not to take. The something that dropped from nowhere was really a someone, Jerry Weintraub, a persuasive, dogged, charming, soft spoken, master of benign bullshit and one helluva producer.

Until Jerry rang my doorbell on this Saturday night at 11:45 PM, and disturbed an interesting discussion that my wife and I were having with our friends, I had not seen Jerry Weintraub since "Oh, God!", the film he produced and I directed twenty years earlier. My first thought was that his car had stalled and he needed a phone, but it turned out that all he needed was me. His new film, "Ocean's 11," was going into production and he was searching for someone to play "Saul Bloom," one of the gang of eleven.

Jerry, being as honest as he needs to be in order to function successfully, did not say that he had come to me because I was the perfect actor for the role. He told me that he had found the perfect actor, Alan Arkin, but Alan had a conflict. Alan had gone to the hospital to undergo minor surgery to repair something that needed repairing. If Jerry could have delayed the film's start, he would not have dropped by. Ever the gentleman, Jerry stayed only long enough to hand me a script, recite the names of the extraordinary cast and director, and apologize for the intrusion.

Many things about the offer pleased me and first among the many was Alan Arkin being cast. Alan and I share a pleasant history that started with his playing a fictionalized version of me in the play "Enter Laughing," and continued with our playing roles in "The Russians Are Coming, The Russians Are Coming", and in the recent past, playing his older brother in "The Slums of Beverly Hills." As an added connection, my wife, in her night club act, sings Alan Arkin's romantically-humorous love song, "I Like You." The words and music of "I Like You" are:

"I like you -cuz u don't make me nervous
I met someone like you before but only once or twice
Once or twice, and not very recently

You'll do; my blood pressure's normal!
I haven't lost no sleep at all–not since Francine
And it's possible for me to concentrate on my work

I'm glad I'm not walking on air
And no trumpets go off in my ear
I don't say to myself, "Get ahold of myself!"
And I don't get a rash when you're near

You're trustworthy
I wouldn't worry if I hadda go away for a few weeks
You don't nag me for money all the time
And one thing I forgot
You're a very good cook
And I certainly loooooove to eat."

The things that pleased me most about the projected remake of "Ocean's 11" was the quality of the script, the juiciness of my role and the actors with whom I'd be working. They were not only talented, but genuine stars who attracted huge crowds whenever they dared to go out in public, and who, I soon learned, were all funsters.

The film was to be shot in Las Vegas and, for one month, I'd be required to live in a suite at the Bellagio and would be paid a salary generous enough to make me feel wanted. George, who played Danny Oceans, the leader of the pack of thieves, was also a major force in convincing all of his star friends that the fun and excitement of working with him, each other and director Steven Soderberg, made it worth accepting less money than they ordinarily would be paid.

During the course of the first few work days, I had the opportunity to perform with, lunch with, and chat with:

Brad Pitt

George Clooney

Don Cheadle, Bernie Mac

Andy Garcia

Elliott Gould

Matt Damon

Scott Caan & Casey Affleck

I did not include Julia Roberts in the impressive list of stars I met, because we never did meet or were even introduced. She didn't work in any of the scenes I was in and unfortunately our paths never crossed, although they came close to crossing when she came out of an elevator in the lobby of the Bellagio to play a scene with Andy Garcia. However, on my way to lunch I did meet her and siezed the opportunity to tell her how absolutely magnificent she was in the film portraying Erin Brockovich.

Julia Roberts

Being twice as old as every member in the company except Elliot Gould, of whom I was only a third older, I didn't get to hang with the guys. They all possessed superhuman ability to get up early, shoot all day, play hard-driving basketball between takes, and be up for long evenings of partying. I used most of my energy to eat, learn my lines, and go to bed. Luckily, I had enough energy to pose for this treasured cast photograph.

One of the lovely things about being in a good movie with good people is the residual good feelings that remain long after the movie's on DVD. I love reading about and rooting for all of their individual successes in films, marriages, love affairs and in aiding good causes. In the case of "Ocean's 11," which was a huge hit, there is also the positive feedback you get from young people, who might not be old enough to have seen you do your thing when it was easier for you to do your thing.

CHAPTER TWENTY-TWO

Whole Foods... What Did I Come Here For?

This morning, leaning against my front door I found a manila envelope containing a script of a very popular TV show for which I had committed to act as a guest star. The fear, or I should say, concern I have

anytime I take on an acting assignment, is about my ability to learn the lines. As I get older, something that used to come easy, has now become a chore.

I read somewhere that the brain is a muscle that requires constant flexing to help it retain new information. I must have read that a long time ago because if I had read it within the past two days, I probably would not remember it.

I'm exaggerating a bit, but every time I think about learning lines, I flash back to a story that was told to me by the film comedian, Leonid Kinsky.

Leonid's friend and fellow actor was Akim Tamiroff, the star of the world-renowned Moscow Art Theatre. I had the good fortune to meet Mr. Tamiroff when I rented his house while working on "The Dinah Shore Television Show."

I so admired the prodigiously talented Akim Tamiroff who, in his time, was the most sought after character actor in Hollywood. He was equally adept at performing in dramas, melodramas and comedies. Among his 156 films, he won a Golden Globe for his performance as Pablo in "For Whom The Bell Tolls."

"For Whom The Bell Tolls"

Mr. Tamiroff's house was located in Beverly Hills at 629 N. Alta Drive.

In the first floor bedroom that my son Rob occupied, hung an oil portrait of Tamiroff's friend, Leonid Kinsky.

During our stay there, Leonid Kinsky told me about his once energetic friend, Akim, becoming a recluse. He spent most of the day sitting in his easy chair and staring at the walls. Leonid tried his best to energize his friend by suggesting they go to a movie theater or take a walk, but to no avail, Akim preferred to sit and stare.

Leonid became so worried about Akim's well-being that he took it upon himself to contact a psychiatric institute and make an appointment for his morose friend. Without telling him where he was going, he managed to convince Akim to go for a drive. When they arrived at the reception desk of the institute Leonid Kinsky was a nervous mess while an aquiescent Akim stood at his side.

When the receptionist, who was filling out an admittance form, asked the applicant, "What is your address?" Leonid was so nervous about the situation he had trouble remembering the address, and after some hesitant, "Uh... uh... uhs," Akim spoke up, "629 N. Alta Drive, Beverly Hills."

"And your telephone number?"

Leonid, who had dialed it a thousand times, again started to stutter, and again Akim came to the rescue and gave them the number.

The receptionist suggested that Akim Tamiroff take a seat in the waiting room and asked Leonid to accompany an attendant, who ushered him to an examination room. For the next fifteen or so minutes Leonid waited impatiently for someone to explain what was going on. Worried about Akim, he started to leave the room, but found the door locked. He rapped at the door four or five times, and when he got no response he started to shout, "The door is locked! Someone open the door!"

An attendant obliged and said, "Calm down, sir, the doctor will be with you in a minute."

"I don't need a doctor... I shouldn't be in here."

"I understand, sir, just calm down and everything will be fine," he said, as he left the room and locked the door.

"Wait... wait," Leonid shouted, "Why you locking the door?"

"Calm down, calm down, sir, you're going to be fine," the attendant shouted and walked down the hall.

Leonid, becoming more and more concerned about the possibility of his friend leaving the hospital and wandering off into traffic, banged on the door, shouting, "Somebody, somebody, let me out of here, let me out of here!"

Once again the attendant came to the door, opened it a crack and shouted, "It will only be another minute before the doctor gets to you."

"I'm not the one who needs to be gotten to. It's my friend who needs help."

A version of the above conversations between a concerned apoplectic Leonid and the attendants went on while, in the waiting room, a calm Akim Tamiroff worried about the whereabouts of his friend.

After thirty minutes of worry, Tamiroff left the waiting room, wandered down the hall and looked into three or four patient's rooms before finding his worn-out apoplectic friend.

The world-renowned Akim Tamiroff moved from Beverly Hills to Palm Springs where, one month shy of his 73rd birthday, he passed away.

Preface

"Forty-nine years ago I wrote and directed a play for Broadway. It was a a Pirandello-like play which I entitled "Something Different." The other day I had an urge to create something different'er than "Something Different."

I came up with the idea of writing unarguably the longest title for the shortest, most satisfying work of romantic fiction, which would garner rave reviews from renowned critics who are almost as smart as Joyce Carol Oates, Ezra Pound, John Gardner, Harold Bloom and Robert Penn Warren, and would be thrilled to read a work which would bring tears to their eyes for a venture which sported the largest font size lettering ever used in any literary endeavor.

I entitled this play:

CHAPTER TWENTY-THREE

"Unarguably The Longest Title For The Shortest, Most Satisfying Work Of Romantic Fiction, Which Would Garner Rave Reviews From Renowned Critics Who Are Almost As Smart As Joyce Carol Oates, Ezra Pound, John Gardner, Harold Bloom And Robert Penn Warren, And Would Be Thrilled To Read A Work Which Would Bring Tears To Their Eyes For A Venture Which Sported The Largest Font Size Lettering Ever Used In Any Literary Endeavor."

CHAP. 1
The Maggios

On Easter Sunday 1945, in the bedroom of their affluent five room apartment on Rochambeau Avenue in the North Bronx, Mr. and Mrs. Joseph & Melody Maggio welcomed their first born, an eight pound, three ounce baby boy.

Because their son was born on this holiest of days, his parents requested that their Priest christen their newborn, "Jesus." The Priest advised them that bearing the name Jesus might be much too heavy a burden for a young lad to carry.

Heeding the advice of their wise Priest, they blended their baptismal names, Joseph & Melody Maggio. They used the J and o from Joseph, the M from Melody, and io from Maggio, giving them the name:

Jomio.

The Birnbaums

On Passover, April the Sixteenth, in the bedroom of Mr. and Mrs Birnbaum's six room apartment on Rochambeau Avenue, in the North Bronx, a beautiful five pound, three ounce baby girl was born.

Because she was born on one of the year's holiest days, her parents considered naming her Bathsheba. Their Rabbi reminded them that Bathsheba was the wife of King David and giving their daughter that name may be too big a burden for her to carry.

Rudy and Liset Birnbaum agreed. They decided to use Bathsheba as her middle name and blend their names. They took the R and u from <u>Ru</u>dy, the L, the i, and the et from <u>Lis</u><u>et</u> and called her:

Ruliet

Throughout her life Ruliet enjoyed telling people how she derived her name. She did not enjoy being spun around by the school's bullies who shouted,
"Make your bets! Ruliet's a Roulette! Ruliet's a Roulette! Ruliet's a Roulette!"

Junior High

At six, Ruliet Birnbaum started public school, where she excelled. Every year, for six years, her report cards boasted A pluses in every subject. At age twelve, Ruliet was an outstanding student.

Her teachers recommended that she be transferred to "Patrick Angelo's Junior High," a school for the gifted. Each day Ruliet would board a bus and travel a half hour to and from school. The weekly fare was fifty cents but no problem for Ruliet's proud, affluent parents.

Guido's Sacrifice

At six, Jomio attended public school and from 1st grade to 6th grade, he received A pluses in all subjects. Jomio's teacher advised Mrs. Maggio that her gifted son should attend "Patrick Angelo Junior High."

When she told her husband that their son would need sixty cents a week for bus fare, Mr. Maggio, a lowly janitor, sighed and said, "Let me think about it." "What's to think about," his wife chided, "Guido, don't you want to give your son a chance to make something of himself?"

"Sure, tell me how I do that?"

"I'll tell you how! Instead of smoking four cigars a day, how about smoking three cigars a day?!"

"I could do that," he smiled.

And that's just what Guido did.

Jomio & Ruliet

"Ooops," Ruliet exclaimed when she dropped her new fountain pen. "Is this your pen?" Jomio asked as he retrieved it. "Yes," she replied, "thank you." Those were the first and only words that Jomio and Ruliet had ever exchanged.

For five long months, in their Algebra class, Jumio had sat directly behind Ruliet and stared at the back of her head. He had fallen in love with every strand of her silky reddish-blond hair.

Walking Home From School Together, Almost

On sunny days when Ruliet opted to save the ten cent bus fare and walk home from school, so would Jomio. Ruliet was usually accompanied by a friend, but Jomio chose to walk alone.

So she would not be aware of his presence, he walked on the opposite side of the street, trailing her by half a block. When Ruliet chose to go home by bus, Jomio managed to board first and find a seat in the very last row. From that vantage point, he would gaze at her and drink in her beauty.

Her Hand, Her Hand, I Held Her Hand

One day at lunch, standing in line at the school's cafeteria, Jomio found himself standing behind Ruliet. She was deeply involved in a conversation with her girlfriend while Jomio stared at her.

He admired how Ruliet's graceful hand reached for a bran muffin. While placing it on her tray, the muffin fell to the ground, and in a flash, Jomio rose to the occasion. This could be his opportunity to meet the love of his life.

He dashed to her side and reached

for the muffin a split second after Ruliet had. Instead of holding her bran muffin, Jomio was holding her hand, the hand he hoped someday to ask for in marriage. He quickly withdrew and mumbled, "S..s.. sorry..I...I..w..w..was trying to p..p..pick up your...m...muffin."

CHAP. 8
Best Buddy Turns Worst Buddy

The only one Jomio ever made privy to his feelings about Ruliet was his best buddy, Buddy Taub, who recommended that Jomio tell Ruliet how he felt about her.

"Look," he goaded, "if you're afraid to tell her, I'll tell her for you."

Jomio reluctantly gave Buddy permission to speak for him and, very soon after, he was sorry that he did.

When Buddy whispered sweetly into Ruliet's ear that she had a secret admirer, she assumed that Buddy was the secret admirer and excitedly gave him a big wet kiss.

At that moment, Jomio had lost the love of his life and acquired a hatred for his buddy, Buddy Taub.

Agreeing To Be Best Man To The Worst Man

Never in a million years, nay, not in two million years, would Jomio ever expect to receive the piece of mail that was delivered to him this day!

Just one month after his worst friend had stolen the love of his life from him,

Buddy Taub, the unmitigated scoundrel, dared to insult Jomio by asking him to act as best man at his betrothal to Ruliet. When he received the embossed wedding invitation, after a gut wrenching scream, he tore the invitation into confetti sized pieces. He then tossed them into a metal basket, lit a match and reduced the 'insult' to ashes.

Jomio stayed awake for three nights contemplating his next move. He ruled out punching Buddy in the nose, running him over with his car or pouring gasoline on him and setting him on fire. He settled for eating nightly

quarts of Rocky-Road
ice cream.

Jomio stayed awake
for two days and two
nights, and on the third
night was awakened
by an angel's voice that
pleaded with him to
come to her wedding.
"It was not Buddy's
idea to send you the
invitation," Ruliet ex-
plained, "or for you to

act as his best man.
It was mine. Jomio,
I still have deep feel-
ings for you. It was
your words," she
whispered, "your
sweet, endearing
words Buddy used,
that caused me to fall
in love and agree to
marry him."

At the wedding
ceremony, Jomio

stood by the groom's side. He looked at neither the Rabbi, the wedding couple, nor the assembled guests. He quietly stared at the back of his eyelids and the moment after he heard the groom's heel smash the wine glass, he fled the Synagogue.

Jomio was saddened to think that it would be the last time he would ever see Ruliet or his worst best-friend, Buddy Taub.

CHAP. 10
This Is The Army Air Force Private Maggio

Until he was assigned for basic training at Fort Valium, Jomio had no idea that, on his aptitude tests, he would receive the highest procedural scores in the class.

And further, he had no idea that these test scores indicated he had an ability to pilot a helicopter.

Just weeks after mastering take-offs, maneuvering and landing these rotor equipped "choppers," he was transferred to Saigon.

There he successfully evacuated scores of refugees from war-torn internment camps and flew them to safe havens.

On his 32nd mission, one of his damaged helicopter blades spun off, sending the plane and Jomio crashing to the ground.

Buddy Taub, Patriot

In searching for a job that would enable him and his wife Ruliet to live a better life, Buddy answered an ad for a job that would secure their financial future. He told his wife that he had filled out an application enlisting her in the United States Army Nurse Corp in Canton, Ohio. Two months later, Lt. Nurse Taub was tending to the wounded in a military field hospital. During her stay, she arranged to have her marriage to Buddy anulled.

All's Well That Ends Weller Than Expected

While tending to one of the twenty patients assigned to her, Lt. Nurse Ruliet was drawn to a heavily bandaged serviceman whose quiet moaning deeply touched her.

She went to his bedside and said, "Now what have we here?"

From behind his facial bandages, she heard a muffled grunt that had a surprisingly happy ring to it. "Did you say something?" she asked.

"Mumiet, Mumiet," he muttered.

"Do you by any chance," she wishfully asked, "mean Ruliet, Ruliet?"
He nodded and 'Mumiet' kissed the bandaged face of her future husband....
a face she would kiss 6,675,837,001 more times in their long and happy life together, raising two girls and twin boys.

The Following Are Seventeen
Short Stories For Which I Have
An Author's Affection

CHAPTER TWENTY-FOUR

SHORT STORY I
Yehudah Benjamin Aronowitz

Every night after work, Yehudah would fix a simple dinner for himself. Tonight it was a boiled potato, two hard-boiled eggs, and a slice of white bread. Whatever it was, he would eat the meal quickly and rush to his desk. If he didn't write down all the random thoughts that had occurred to him that day, he would consider it a day wasted. This day he wrote:

- He that pays the piper, calls the tune.
- Death cancels everything but truth.
- Prejudice is being down on something you are not up on.
- Never trouble till trouble troubles you.
- Nothing in excess.
- He who excuses himself, accuses himself.
- Better to idle well than to work poorly.
- Go to law for a sheep and lose your cow.

He added a new page to the immense stack that had been growing for thirty-nine years. Tonight he would bundle up a sheath of papers and tomorrow he would dispatch it to a publisher. He dipped a newly sharpened quill into the inkwell and on this, his fiftieth birthday, he wrote the letter that, long ago, he had promised himself he would write.

My Dear Mr. Bartlet,

Enclosed please find some thoughts I have jotted down.
I hope you will find some of them suitable for publication.

Very Truly Yours,

Yehudah Benjamin Aronowitz

A fortnight later he received the following reply.

Dear Mr. Aronowitz,

I much enjoyed your "thoughts" and with your permission I would like to include all of them in a new edition that I am readying for publication. As I am sure you are aware, we do not pay a great deal of money for bright sayings, but I daresay that you will derive a measure of satisfaction in seeing your name in a book that includes Shakespeare, Samuel Johnson, La Rochefoucauld, and Aristotle. If you accept our offer a contract will be sent to you for your signature.

Admiringly, John Bartlett

Yehudah Benjamin signed the contract but he regretted initialing the addendum to the contract which read:

Because we intend to include 150 of your bright sayings in our Christmas edition we feel strongly that using your full name, Yehudah Benjamin Aronowitz, would hurt sales in growing anti-semitic communities. One of our editors suggested we use only your last name, Aronowitz, and shorten it to Aron. I pointed out that Aron suggests Aaron, old testament biblical, and I fear it will defeat our purpose. So, we will go forward if you grant us permission to modify your name to Anon. I'm sure you will agree that Anon is both elegant and ambiguous.

Dear John

June 6, 1999

Dear John,

This is the most difficult letter I have written in my life. I considered not writing it, but I remembered what you always told me, "We are nothing if we are not honest."

So, dear John, I am taking your advice and being honest. I hurts me so, but I realize that there is no other way. After much soul searching, I have decided to call off our wedding.

I know you are saying to yourself, "Why does she wait to do this till three days before the ceremony?" John, when I explain, you'll realize that you are partly to blame. Last week after dinner at Mercurio's, which, by the way, was delicious—and I know how expensive it was even though my menu didn't have the prices on it. I know what real caviar costs and I really dug in, didn't I? Well, that night, as always, you were too generous, and it is because of your generosity that I am calling off our relationship.

I don't know how many times you have said to me that everything you have is mine. I always believed you meant it, but I don't believe that I ever believed that I believed you. When you said that after we were married, that I would be an equal partner in your dry-cleaning store, I believed you. But, that night at the restaurant, you went too far. I was only joking when you were paying the bill and I said, "Is your wallet mine, too?" And to prove your point, you insisted I take it and keep it. Well, as you know, I didn't keep it but sent it back to you in that insured package. John, you should never have let me take that wallet home. You see, I looked through it and found a picture of you and your uncle Dominic, the one of you on the beach in Maui. You did tell me about him, but you never mentioned what an extremely attractive man he is.

I showed the picture to my mother, and she noticed that on the back he had written "Dominic Saletero at 63 and my nephew John at 39." Mom and I both agree that he was the best looking sixty-three-year-old that we'd ever seen. Mom insisted I give him a call to invite him to our wedding, and I did. He was very nice and said that you had sent him a snapshot of me. He told me I was very pretty, and I told him what a generous man you are and that I got to see his picture because you had given me your wallet. I must say, John, you and your uncle Dominic are so much alike.

He said that if I get out of my commitment to you, everything he had would be mine, including the hotel he owns in Maui. Yesterday, Dominic wired money for airfare and Mom and I are at the airport now. We leave for Hawaii in ten minutes, so I don't have time to write more, I'll send you a postcard when I get there.

I hope you're not too angry with me, but you did say anything you had was mine and that I could have whatever I want. Well, I want your Uncle Dominic. Thank you, and God bless you. I know he will, John.

Sincerely,

Mary

P.S. You won't find anything missing from your wallet except the stamp I used for this letter, and now you have that back too.

Lance & Gwendolyn
A MODERN FAIRY TALE

Lance Bensen pushed the button for the 20th floor, then when he saw her coming down the hall, he quickly pressed the door-open button. His heart stopped and his eyelids locked open as he watched the apparition coming toward the elevator.

"Guinevere," he muttered, looking at the real-life embodiment of an illustration of Lady Guinevere that adorned the cover of his copy of "Lancelot and Guinevere." Lady Guinevere, the willowy figure to whom, twenty years ago on his thirteenth birthday, he had secretly plighted his troth. The long, filmy gown Lady Guinevere wore allowed only a glimpse of her dainty sandaled feet. He had fantasized so many times that her legs would look exactly like the long, perfectly sculpted ones that now made their way toward him. She glided into the elevator, smiled, and whispered a "Thank you" so deeply sensual that he started to perspire.

"What floor, please?" he asked, praying it would be the highest.

"Eighty-one, please."

"Incredible!" he blurted out.

"I beg your pardon?"

"Uh, incredible," he stammered, pushing the button, "that man has the ability to build something eighty-one stories high."

She smiled and nodded. He checked the floor indicator and saw he had less than seventy floors to confess his undying love for her.

"Hello, my name is Lance Bensen. I'm an attorney at Harris, Reissman & Bensen. Our offices are on the twentieth floor. You may think me mad but I assure you I am a sane and responsible person. A moment ago, when you approached the elevator, my heart stopped. Do you believe in love at first sight?"

"Well, frankly," she whispered softly, "I never, ever thought I would."

"But you do?"

She smiled and nodded.

He could not believe that she had not slapped his face, much less answered the question the way she had.

"On my eleventh birthday," Lance replied rapidly, "My father gave me an illustrated edition of 'Lancelot and Guinevere' and I fell in love with the illustration of Lady Guinevere. To this day I am haunted by that image. Am I frightening you?"

"On the contrary, I know the book you're describing. It's a black book with a colored inset of them on the cover."

"Yes, yes, by Lawrence Dempsey," he continued, his enthusiasm mounting, "and there is an illustration of Guinevere and Lancelot at the beginning..."

"...of the third chapter! I have that book! What an amazing coincidence. What did you say your name was?"

"Lance, Lance Bensen."

"Lance! No!" she said, laughing.

"My mother gave me the book," he answered, glancing at the indicator and noting that he had but a few floors to win the hand of the fair maiden.

"This may sound infantile, but I have judged every girl I have ever met against the image of that glorious woman. I can admit it now, but it may be the reason I'm not married. You think I'm crazy, don't you?"

"Sir, I am probably one of the few people who wouldn't think you're crazy." She smiled at him with a warmth and understanding that sent a rush of blood through his body. "I can't believe you're saying this to me."

"You're not angry?"

"How could I be angry at a kindred spirit?" she asked.

She had called him a kindred spirit! He could barely keep himself from grabbing her hand and pressing it to his lips.

"That magical illustration," she continued," had the same profound effect on me. I too was forever looking for a man who resembled Sir Lancelot. I knew it was silly, but..."

The elevator slowed, and he knew he must say something that would keep this encounter from being a brief one. The doors opened and before he could think of what to say she stepped off the elevator, turned to him, smiled and asked hopefully, "Do you have a moment?"

A moment? he thought, *how about an eternity?*

"Yes," he said, attempting to sound casual. "Um, my first meeting isn't for half an hour."

"Well then," Lady Guinevere said beckoning him with her finger, "follow me."

'To the ends of the earth,' he muttered to himself.

He followed her down the hall, lagging back far enough to enjoy the graceful sway of her hips. She stopped at the office door, where scripted gold letters informed him that the name of his fantasy woman was Gwendolyn Lord.

She opened the door and, with what he perceived as a devilish smile, bade him enter. She glided to her desk, picked up a large silver frame and handed it to him.

"Guinevere and Lancelot from the book," he said, shaking his head in disbelief. "You had it framed."

Gwendolyn picked up another frame from her desk and gave it to him. It seemed to be an exact duplicate of the illustrated page.

"You framed two of these?"

"Look at them closely," she asked.

"I am. This one is a photograph of the illustration."

"You're very kind, but that's me and my husband, Marvin. It's our wedding picture taken three weeks ago. Doesn't Marvin look like Sir Lancelot in the illustration?"

Reluctantly, he admitted that Marvin was the spitting image of the handsome knight. Lance congratulated her on her marriage, bade her farewell and walked sadly out of her office and out of her life.

Though Lance and Gwendolyn worked in the same building they did not see each other until two years later, when Gwendolyn walked into the offices of Harris, Reissman & Bensen and asked Lance if he would handle her divorce.

My husband," she explained, "is the very embodiment of what Sir Lancelot was really like, a medieval, male chauvinist, womanizing schmuck."

Lance and Gwendolyn were married a year and a half later and were considered by all, themselves included, to be a relatively happy couple.

Mr. Gutman and Dr. Magic

"Sir, is this some sort of gimmick?"

"I assure you it isn't, Mister...?

"Gutman."

"Mr. Gutman, there is no gimmick to my offer."

"It sure sounds gimmicky."

"What sounds gimmicky?"

"Well, for one thing, your name, Dr. Magic."

"It's my professional name. What else sounds gimmicky?"

"The offer itself. You guarantee an awful lot of things for three hundred dollars."

"Two hundred-ninety-nine dollars."

"Who are you trying to fool? Why not make it three hundred?"

"Because what I have to offer is worth two hundred and ninety-nine dollars and not a penny more."

"How do I use this stuff?"

"It all depends on what you want to do, Mr. Gutman."

"Let's say, Doc, that I'm interested in everything you claim it can do."

"I thought you might be. Alright, get a pencil and piece of paper and write down what I tell you."

"Isn't there a brochure?"

"If I had a brochure printed, it would bring up the cost. Are you ready?"

"I guess. Shoot!"

"Well, for baldness, you take a tablespoonful every day with meals and before retiring rub a spoonful of it into your scalp. For lower back pain, rub a teaspoon of the formula into the troubled area. For hearing loss, one drop in each ear daily. For a sinus condition, two drops into each nostril on awakening. For jock itch and athlete's foot, a half cup added to your washing machine's rinse cycle. For constipation, one tablespoon poured into your morning juice, unless you are also treating your baldness, in which case, just add a quarter teaspoon to your baldness dose. For dry, itchy skin, three capfuls dropped into your warm bath. For lip herpes, dip a Q-tip into the formula and apply gently to the sore every hour for six hours and repeat the following day.

"For failing eyesight," he continued, "one drop in each eye daily until the condition reverses itself. For hemorrhoids, apply directly to the swelling with a soaked cotton ball and hold until relief comes—usually in six to nine minutes. This formula will not cure venereal disease, cancer, Parkinson's or AIDS and I'd be a fraud if I told you it would."

"I'll take it!"

"You won't be sorry, Mr. Gutman."

"What if I need a refill?"

"You'll never need one. This gallon will permanently cure all the illnesses I enumerated."

"What if I'm not satisfied?"

"Mr.Gutman, only a malcontent would not be satisfied."

"I am a malcontent."

"A malcontent? Really? Hmmm, Mr. Gutman, why don't you try taking a small gulp of my formula right now."

Mr. Gutman swallowed a dose of the magic elixir and waited expectantly.

"So, Mr. Gutman, what's the verdict?"

"It works!" he announced gleefully, handing Dr. Magic a check. "I'm so pleased!"

"Hold on, Gutman! A dollar more please!"

"But you said two hundred and ninety-nine..."

"Yes, but that was before I discovered that my formula would cure malcontentment."

Mr. Gutman was more than happy to pay the extra dollar.

The People vs. DeMarco

"State your name."

"Anthony DeMarco, Your Honor."

"Are you represented by counsel?"

"I'm gonna be my own counsel."

"How do you plead?"

"Well, I don't know. What's better, guilty with an explanation or not guilty with no explanation?"

"Are you sure you don't want the advice of counsel? The court can appoint one."

"No, I'll be alright. I'm gonna plead guilty with an explanation. What I did was perfectly understandable if you know the circumstances. Even you, Judge, woulda done what I did."

"May we hear what you did?"

"Certainly, Your Honor, that's what we're here for, right?"

"Right, Mr. DeMarco, continue."

"A little justice tempered with mercy, that's all I'm asking for. Well, Your Honor, what happened was this. Last night, about midnight, I hear a scream that knocked me outta my bed. It's like no scream I ever heard before, a real blood curdler, like in a slasher movie. Anyway, I pick myself off the floor, and I'm looking at my girlfriend, Viola, who lives with me—we're engaged, by the way. She's yelling at the top of her lungs and pointing to the window. I run to the window and look out, and there's nothing there but a big moon and some trees. She keeps screaming and pointing, so I grab her by the shoulders and shake her, but she keeps hollering and pointing, so I do what anybody would do to bring her out of it. I give her a whack on the cheek."

"Hard enough to cause the abrasions that are described in the police report?"

"Oh, no way, Your Honor. I used an open hand. Her cheek wasn't even red. Anyway, she starts blubbering that she was attacked by a big bat."

"A big bat, Mr. DeMarco?"

"Yeah, a big bat, I knew you'd be dubious. Your Honor, she said it looked like Dracula."

I tell her she had a nightmare, but she keeps insisting that Dracula was in the room and bit her, and she's afraid he'll come back and bite her again. She says that if he bites you a couple of times, you turn into a vampire. I tell her she's nuts, but she shows me her neck and you know what, Your Honor?"

"Nooo, tell me."

"There's, like, two small hickeys there. I tell her it wasn't Dracula that bit her but one of Spunky's fleas. Her dog, Spunky, sleeps with us. She gets real insulted and screams, 'I just gave him his flea bath.' 'Maybe you missed a couple, I yelled back.'"

"Mr. DeMarco, where is this story going?"

"Right to the truth, Your Honor. Shall I continue?"

"Please do."

"Well, with the help of a triple dose of NyQuil and a couple of lullabies–I'm a singer, ya know."

"No, I didn't, Mr. DeMarco."

"I go by the name of Val Volino. I did a couple of commercials for Valvoline motor oil. That's where I got my stage name, Val Volino."

"Can we get back to your explanation, Mr. DeMarco?"

"Right, Your Honor, I'll try to make it fast. I know you got a lot of criminals waiting in the bullpen. So, there we are, sound asleep, and I wake up to take a leak–is it alright to say that? I don't mean no disrespect."

"None taken, please continue."

"Thank you, Your Honor. So, I'm coming back from the crapper and am I in for a surprise. This damn Dracula that Viola's been screaming about, you're not going to believe this, Your Honor, but there he is hovering over our bed."

"You're right, Mr. DeMarco, I don't believe it."

"I told you you wouldn't. I don't blame you for being skeptical. I never believed in vampires either, but I'm a believer now. I tell you, I went berserk. This Dracula guy is about to give my Viola another one of his famous vampire bites and I'm scared that she's gonna get sucked into his world, so I grab my baseball bat–you know, I used to play on the Valvoline company team..."

"No, I didn't."

"Oh yeah, left field, I'll tell you about that later. Anyway, I swing from the heels and I clip this SOB right in the chops and he takes off like a big-ass bird, right out the window. I think I knocked out one of his fangs. Unluckily, on my follow-through, the bat clipped Viola on her cheek, and that's how she ends up with those abrasions she got there in the police report. Well, that's it, Your Honor. That's why I plead guilty with an explanation."

"And *that* is your explanation."

"Yes, Your Honor. No good?"

"Unless you have a better one, Mr. DeMarco, I'm afraid we are going to have to arraign you."

"Ok, how about this one? I'm at work and I start to get these flu symptoms, you know, aches and fever, so I go home early and I find Viola taking a shower with my cousin Carmine. He's singing 'April Showers' and soaping her up and she's laughing and having a wonderful time, and when they see me, you know what they do, Your Honor?"

"I'm counting on you to tell me, Mr. DeMarco."

"Nothing. They don't do nothing. Carmine just keeps on soaping and singing and Viola keeps on laughing. They invite me in. They're shameless. I don't know if it was the flu or the hot stream from the shower, but I could feel my blood boiling. I had to do something. So, I open the shower door, and yank them out of there... that's all I did. Your Honor, I know you're wondering about how Viola got those bruises you saw."

"You've read my mind."

"Well, they were both soaped up, and when they stepped onto the tile floor, they slipped and went flying. On her way down, Viola hit her cheek on the towel rack and Carmine fell right on my fist—I admit it was clenched, and lucky it was there or he would have crashed into the toilet bowl. You like that explanation any better, Your Honor?"

"A little. How accurate is it?"

"Very... except for a few details, Your Honor."

"I'd appreciate hearing those few details."

"Well, I ordered both of them out of my house, and while they were getting dressed I lectured them on loyalty and trust, and I emphasized my disappointment in their behavior."

"How did you do that?"

"By whacking them with my nephew's Wiffle Ball bat. Lucky for them my Louisville Slugger wasn't handy. I tell you, Judge, I was boiling. Truth is, I'm still pretty hot."

"In that case, Mr. DeMarco, to help you cool off I'm giving you ninety days in the county jail."

"Good idea, Judge, but I could cool off in thirty."

"I'd prefer you use the full ninety."

"Then ninety it is! You're the Judge."

"Thank you, Mr. DeMarco."

"Anytime."

Geoff and Kurt

"I beg your pardon, sir, but what is that you're eating? My wife and I are about to order and that dish of yours looks awfully good."

"Ach, thank you. Is goot. Hassenpfeffer, uh, rabbit. See on the menu, Lapin Provencal, very goot flavors. You are American?"

"British."

"Ah, that is nice. We are from Germany, Etta and Kurt Kessler."

"How do you do? Alice and Geoff Hardwicke here."

"How do you do, Mr. And Mrs. Hardwicke? My wife Emma and I, we go to England Tuesday. You know Harrow?"

"Well, how about that, darling? The Kesslers are going to Harrow."

"You are familiar with Harrow, Mr. Hardwicke?"

"Call me Geoff. Are we ever. Harrow is where Alice and I make our home."

"Unbelievable! There is where I go to visit."

"That is a jolly coincidence. Have you been there before?"

"Oh no, but my father spoke often of Harrow. During the World War he dropped bombs on it."

"You don't say!"

"Ah yes, twelve times."

"Alice, isn't that unbelievable? Mr. Kessler's father bombed our hometown twelve times."

"Please to call me Kurt."

"Kurt, where are you folks from? Not Dresden, by any chance?"

"No, no. We are from Dortmund."

"That would be too big a coincidence. You see, in 1944 my Dad dropped firebombs on Dresden."

"Your father dropped bombs on Dresden? No, I don't believe it."

"It's true. His squadron sent the whole city up in flames."

"I know, I know, that is the reason why my family moved to Dortmund."

"Alice, isn't this an astonishing coincidence?"

"Mind-boggling!"

"Mr. Hardwicke- I'm sorry, Geoff—may I buy you a bottle of wine?"

"I was about to ask you that, Kurt."

"Ach, but I ask first!"

"Ah yes, but we won the war!"

"And you win again. Alright, Geoff, you buy the wine."

Hampa Ham

Every Sunday from the age of one, Corey Hammersberg-Carter and his parents drove home from their modest home in Larchmont, New York, to Grandfather Charles Hammersberg's estate in Holly Hills, Connecticut. At the weekly family dinner, Corey, starting at the age of two, addressed his maternal grandfather as "Hampa Ham." The old man found it amusing and enjoyed it so much that he insisted all his grandchildren address him as Hampa Ham. The older ones balked, complaining that it was "babyish." They were quickly reminded by their parents that Grandpa was very old and very wealthy and it was in their best interests to call their grandfather whatever he wished to be called.

Except for the food, Corey could recall many things about these Sunday rituals that he didn't like. He didn't like his cousins, or listening to the same inspirational speech his grandfather insisted on delivering, a tedious, seven minute lecture before dessert was served.

To fight boredom, Corey started timing the speech with the stopwatch his grandfather had given him for Christmas. Each week, Corey would try to guess how many seconds under or over it would be. As the years went on, the speech took longer and longer and by the time Corey was fifteen, it ran close to nine minutes. Corey knew the speech backward and forward and had once recited it backward to his shocked and furious parents. They withheld his allowance that week and forbade him to ever do it again.

Corey knew that his grandfather was a multi-multimillionaire and that all his relatives, including Corey's father, were after his money. On the Sundays when they visited Hampa Ham, his father would insist that his mother wear her most attractive dress.

"Cynthia darling," he remembered his father saying, "why don't you wear your darker lipstick? It enhances your smile."

When Mr. Hammersberg's youngest daughter's boyfriend, Paul, asked for Cynthia's hand in marriage he received permission and an admonition.

"Young man, I will know by the bloom on my daughter's cheeks and the smile on her lips just how loving and caring a husband you are."

From that day forward, Paul was careful not to do anything that would keep his wife's lips from smiling or her cheeks from blooming.

It was fortunate that Paul liked Cynthia well enough that being a good and thoughtful husband was not much of a burden.

At his eighty-fifth birthday party, Hampa Ham, who for five years had not delivered his famous Hammersberg address, decided once again to bore his loyal family with a slower and muted version.

Corey, who could still recite it backward, found himself paying rapt attention. The speech, because of the old man's infirmities, timed out at nineteen minutes, but the salient points were still there:

"Know what you want and go for it."

"Timidity will get you nowhere."

"People who are afraid to ask questions are people who live in the dark."

"If there is someone who has something you want, ask him how he got it, and then go out and do what he did."

When the old man promised that it was the last time that he would make his Sunday speech, he was met by a chorus of insincere voices urging him to reconsider and assuring him how much they loved hearing his speech. While the sycophantic din was at its apex, Corey asked Hampa Ham if he might have a few minutes alone with him.

Corey's parents and relatives watched him as he sat on the veranda and chatted with his grandfather. No one could hear what was being said but the amount of laughter Corey provoked and the manner in which the two shook hands and embraced was quite disturbing to all the heirs.

The following Sunday, Hampa Ham passed away.

The reading of the will was held in the library of the Holly Hills mansion. Most of Charles Hammersberg's relatives were openly angry at what they learned. One nephew sounded off at the grievous injustice that had been done to him by that "selfish old bastard who bored us to shit every Sunday preaching that damn sermon."

Cynthia was saddened by her father's death, but quite pleased at her son's good fortune. She did wonder why her father had chosen to award Corey more money then he did them. In the quiet of their bedroom, Paul insisted that it was they who were responsible for their son's windfall inheritance. It was they who had taught him his good manners and courteous behavior. Cynthia suggested that perhaps Corey himself played a part in winning the huge inheritance. She reminded Paul how her son had utterly endeared himself to her father when he had mangled the pronunciation of his name.

"Nobody in the history of the universe ever gave a person so large an inheritance for accidentally inventing a silly nickname like Hampa Ham," Paul argued. "It was the upbringing that did it."

In fact, it was neither the painstaking parenting nor the cute baby talk that tilted the scales in Corey's favor. It was the admission he made to his grandfather on that fateful last Sunday. He had admitted to his Hampa Ham how, when he was young, he had dreaded coming to the Sunday dinners, knowing that he would have to suffer through a boring lecture before getting his cake and ice cream. He told how, to keep himself amused, he memorized The Hammersberg's Address–backward. He demonstrated his ability to do this and was surprised when his grandfather laughed and asked him to do it again.

Corey then admitted that the speech had absolutely no meaning to him "until now."

"When I heard you speak today," Corey said, "I felt you were talking to me. I'm eighteen now and I know what I want to do with my life. I want to be like you, Hampa Ham, a multi-multimillionaire. In your speech you say, 'Timidity will get you nowhere!'... and 'You live in the dark if you don't ask questions,' and 'If there is someone who has what you want, ask them how they got it and do what they did.'"

"Well, Hampa Ham, I'm asking. How did you get to become a multi-multimillionaire?"

His grandfather, rasping and wheezing, told of his Uncle Zeke, a man he much admired.

"My Uncle Zeke was a smart man who went to South America, discovered a tin mine and became rich manufacturing cans. When I turned seventeen my uncle asked me what I wanted for my birthday and I told him, 'I want to be rich like you.' I asked him to give me a hundred thousand dollars and he did. I invested in a lot of things, the Coca-Cola Company, blue-chip stocks and long-term federal bonds. I made a fortune."

Corey, inspired by this story, shouted out, "Then that's what I'll do. Grandpa, for my birthday you can give me money to start my business?"

"Corey, you are a smart boy! Come by tomorrow and I'll give you a check for a hundred thousand dollars."

"Grandpa, I really appreciate your kindness but... uh..."

The old man shook his head and said that he was pleased that his grandson had learned something from the lecture and requested Corey to say it backward "one more time." When Corey finished, the old man laughed, kissed his grandson on the cheek. He pondered for a moment and then quietly asked,

"Son, when you said you appreciated my kindness you added a but... uh... what were you about to say?"

"I was about to say that the hundred thousand dollars your Uncle Zeke gave you, would today be worth more like..."

"I know, I know," his grandfather laughed, "a million dollars... and that's what you'll get!"

"I appreciate that, Grandpa, but your arithmetic is a little off—the truth is, a hundred thousand dollars back then would, today, be more like ten million dollars!"

"Corey, I can't tell you how pleased and proud I am to have a grandson who takes after me."

With that, Hampa Ham took from his pocket an envelope, and with a big smile on his face said,

"Here, my boy, is a ten million dollar check that I was sure you'd ask for."

Xavier

Once Xavier Cobbler made up his mind to do something, he would take a deep breath and inevitably decide to do something else. Once deciding to do something else, nothing could stop him from considering an alternate activity.

Today Xavier zeroed in on a most exciting project, rolled up his sleeves, and noticed a smudge of dirt on his forearm, which he took to the sink to wash away.

There was something about running water that started his mind whirring. So many of his most creative schemes had come to him in the shower or while he was urinating. As he scrubbed away at the stubborn Magic Marker stain on his arm, a new undertaking started to form and it excited him. Nothing in this world could dissuade him from seeing this work to completion, unless there was a major sporting event on television. He found one, the state bowling championship, live from Raleigh, North Carolina.

As he watched the bowling ball roll down the lane and strike the pins, he jumped up and shouted, "I've got it!" And he did have it, an idea for a great new board game—Procrastination.

He raced to the telephone, snatched it off the cradle and punched in 411.

"The telephone number for the Milton Bradley Company, please."

Xavier was about to dial the Milton Bradley number when he remembered his ten o'clock appointment with Dr. Brunch.

Sitting in his psychiatrist's waiting room, Xavier fiddled with the slip of paper on which he had jotted down the phone number of the Milton Bradley Company.

'417-555-1141,' he mused, '*if split in two's would become 41-75-55-11-41, which I have a strong hunch would be the winning numbers for tomorrow's Powerball Lottery.*'

He checked his watch and realized that if he rushed, he would have just enough time to buy a ticket just before the lottery machines were shut down. Bolting from the waiting room he pledged that, starting tomorrow, he would spend all of his time and energy working with Dr. Brunch on getting to the root cause of his procrastination problem.

The following night, Xavier watched the evening news and learned that his hunch was right, 41-75-55-11-41 were the winning numbers and the payoff was fifty-six million dollars.

"Fifty-six million dollars!" he mumbled over and over again.

Xavier, who did not consider himself a religious man, clasped his hands and fell to his knees.

"Lord," he said, looking heavenward, "from this day forward, when I'm on my way to buy a lottery ticket, I vow never to stop at a deli for a hot dog with mustard and sauerkraut... unless I am really, *really* hungry."

Caz

"Ah, Caz, my good and dear friend. I trust that you are well–you look fit."

"But for a dull ache in my groin, I can truthfully say that I am in the best shape of my life."

"And how do you find your new lady friend?"

"Smashing and available at all hours."

"As I would expect. What is her name?"

"I am not sure. I meant to ask her last night, but I was distracted."

"Well, as Shakespeare says, 'What's in a name?' By the way, Gina and I are picnicking tomorrow. Care to join us?"

"I would adore that, Victorio, but I have this bothersome groin thing."

"How long have you had it?"

"I believe it started immediately after Valentine's Day."

"Caz, Valentine's Day was six months ago. Have you seen a physician?"

"Why would I?"

"My God, Caz, if I had a pain that long, I'd want to know what was causing it."

"I know that I carried this rather heavy young lady up a long flight of marble stairs... perhaps... no, no. I already had the pain before I lifted her off the floor."

"Why don't you see a doctor?"

"Because I know this pain will go away... as they all do. The body has a way of healing itself..."

"Caz, in case your body does not know the way, my cousin Dr. Roncalo is an excellent diagnostician. You should get at least one professional opinion."

———————————

"Dr. Roncalo, I cannot believe what you are suggesting. Except for that one little groin pain, I feel wonderful."

"But you say the pain is constant and getting worse daily."

"But it's not unbearable."

"It will become so unless you accept what must be done."

"Doctor, what you are describing is so drastic. Is there not a pill? Or perhaps you could operate. I hear there are new surgical procedures—"

"There are no procedures for your condition, and what I'm recommending is not that extreme."

"Not that extreme, you say? Giving up sex is not that extreme??"

"Signor, please do not shout. I did not ask you to give up sex, I merely recommended that you cut back—"

"To three times a night and no morning or afternoon dalliances on Sunday?!" he shouted. "Doctor, that to me is giving it up! I cannot live that way. I would rather suffer the pain."

"It is your life, Signor."

"Thank you, Doctor, I am glad you agree."

Casanova died on February 14, 1798. Last week, on the two-hundredth anniversary of his death, an autopsy was performed and the pain in his groin was still measurable.

Dial 411 for Legal Smut

"Hello, information? I'd like to place an obscene phone call but I do not want to go beyond the bounds of good taste."

"Sir, you want a nine-hundred number."

"Oh, I don't want to talk obscenely to a stranger. The nine-hundred number people are the ones who do that for a living, aren't they?"

"Yes, they are."

"Well, that won't do. I want to talk to my girlfriend."

"I see. Well, then I suggest you call her."

"I intend to, but how can I be certain I won't be cut off for using unacceptable language."

"I'm sure I don't know."

"Well, who does know?"

"I'll connect you with my supervisor."

" Yes, can I help you?"

"I hope so. I'd like to place an obscene phone call, and I was wondering if you have a list of words or phrases that have been ruled obscene. I wouldn't want to run afoul of the law while chatting with my girlfriend."

"Well, sir, what did you intend to say to her?"

"Well, I dreamed of her crotch last night and I'd like to tell her about it."

"I don't think there will be a problem there."

"I'd also like to inform her that I would like to nurse on her breasts until she moans in ecstasy."

"Breast is an acceptable word."

"Good. Then I'd like to say a few things about her vagina."

"Such as?"

"Oh, how I'd like to fondle it for awhile..."

"I see no problem there."

"Oh good. Can I say 'cock'?"

"AT and T would prefer you say penis, but if we are not monitoring the context, 'cock' might be acceptable. You see, 'cock' could be referring to a male rooster."

"Oh, that's great. I want to use cock a few times."

"Well, sir, I wouldn't overdo it if I were you."

"Are you speaking professionally or aesthetically?"

"Aesthetically. The word would lose its impact if it were overused."

"Oh, I wouldn't overuse it, but I feel that just saying it once wouldn't be as effective as repeating it four or five times, in sort of a rhythmic way, like Vachel Lindsay's poem about the jungle."

"I see what you're getting at."

"Well, thank you, you've been a big help. I guess I'll just go ahead and make my obscene phone call."

"I word of caution, Mister, uh, did you say your name?"

"I don't think so. It's Gilbert, Gilbert Corona."

"Zina Hathaway here."

"How do you do, Mrs. Hathaway?"

"*Miss* Hathaway. What I was saying, Mr. Corona... Corona, is that a Spanish name?"

"Yes, my father's family is from Argentina."

"Ah. As I was saying, Mr. Corona, if you're thinking of using words in addition to 'crotch,' 'vagina,' 'breast,' or 'cock'..."

"Well, I may. In the heat of conversation, other words may pop into my mind. I do know a lot of provocative words."

"In that case, Mr. Corona, it might be advisable to have them checked out."

"What words should I try to avoid?"

"There are so many of them..."

"For instance?"

"Well, offhand, 'prick' out of context, 'sucking' in some contexts... as I say, there are so many of them. I'd like to be more helpful, Mr. Corona, but I don't have the time right now. Look, why don't you call me later at 212-555-1123. I'll compile a comprehensive list of all the words and phrases you should avoid using."

"What time shall I call?"

"Well, I leave here at 5, and if traffic is normal, I'll be home at six."

"That is so nice of you, Miss Hathaway."

"I'm always happy to help someone who shows such sensitivity. I'll expect your call at six. That's 1-212-555-1123. If I'm not home by that time, just keep calling back until I pick up. Do you have a redial feature?"

"I do."

"Good. Until six... *Gilberto*."

How Could This Happen

What had he done? Was he being punished for his sins? What sins? He had always lived according to the rules, he had towed the line, done to others as he had wanted done to him. Was he being singled out, or was this horror also being visited on others? He was afraid to move. A sharp pain of hunger stabbed at his gut. Bread, a tiny crust of bread was all he needed, or a drop of water, where would he find either? Maybe under the kitchen table, but how would he get to the kitchen? He was flat on his back, something he always dreaded might happen to him. He strained to raise his head but couldn't. He felt strangely disconnected. He had no feeling in his legs. He looked down his body to see them. What had happened to his legs? Oh god! Most of them were gone—only two were left, and what a strange shape they had taken! It was imperative that he get off his back and find his family. With a herculean effort, he rolled over and landed on the floor. The kitchen! He must crawl into the kitchen. But how could he crawl anywhere with just two legs? He strained and strained and finally pulled himself upright. He looked toward the kitchen and took heart. There was his whole family, crawling toward him!

Dozens and dozens of his siblings encircled him, warily keeping their distance. They seemed to be so small and so far away. Finally, his mother or his father, he was never able to tell one from the other, scurried up the leg of the kitchen table and stared at him.

"Mom, or Dad, what has happened to me?"

"My son," one of them chirped, "you are no longer one of us."

"Oh dear god, tell me, what am I?"

"Gregor darling," the other parent cried, "you have turned into a... a Kafka!"

Too Damned Handsome

Dino Romano did not stand a chance. His mother was a Victoria's Secret model and his father, who died in a demolition derby in Hackensack six months before he was born, was once described as a handsome version of Robert Redford.

Lying in his carriage, little blond-haired Dino heard, but never understood, the hundreds of compliments that came his way.

"Mrs. Romano," a neighbor cooed, "that baby is the most beautiful baby I've ever seen in my life."

In the park, when he was old enough to play in the sandbox, he began to sense that something was going on that involved him.

Dozens of times he heard people say to his mother, "Madam, I have seen gorgeous children in my life, but your girl is really out-of-this-world gorgeous!"

Informed that Dino was a boy, they would shake their heads in disbelief. One woman asked, "Are you sure?"

As a child, he was too pretty to be a boy and as a teenager he was too pretty to be a man. His eyelashes were the envy of every mooning female who had ever stared into his lavender eyes.

All through high school and his one semester in trade school he was urged to become an actor, or at least a model.

"A male or female model," a cruel friend suggested, "you'd never be out of work."

By the time he was twenty three, he had tried everything and had failed miserably at each endeavor.

While Mother Nature had blessed him with extraordinary looks, she thought to balance the scale by giving him no discernible talent or personality, and just enough intelligence to experience frustration, pain and anger.

'*Why,*' he asked himself, '*does everyone expect so much of me just because I'm so goddamned handsome?*'

He lived up to his potential, but no one would accept that. Dozens of girls fell in love with him on sight, and all were disappointed to learn he was not only content to drive a beer truck, but enjoyed it. After too many years of failing to live up to his looks, he decided that he'd had it. He didn't ask to be born with devastatingly handsome features and he was not going to accept his fate a day longer.

One afternoon, after being told by a salesgirl that he was "soooo, soooo beautiful," he randomly chose one of the dozens of plastic surgeons listed in the Beverly Hills phone book.

"Dr. Cutler," he pleaded, "what can you do for me?"

The doctor examined a face that he had many times tried to sculpt onto his needier patients.

"Unless you are running from the law," the doctor said, shaking his head, "why would you want to change your face?"

"It doesn't go with my personality."

"Well, then, I suggest you try changing your personality because your face is perfection and I never tamper with perfection."

When Dino asked Dr. Cutler if he could recommend someone who might be willing to help him, the doctor angered him by recommending a psychiatrist. He visited every plastic surgeon listed, and all had similar reasons for rejecting his business. He became so depressed that he found it difficult to get out of bed. One morning he called in sick and told his supervisor that he would not be coming to work for awhile.

His depression made it impossible for him to function. One afternoon, he stood stock-still in the parking lot of a mini-mall, unable to decide where to lunch. For fifteen minutes, while vacillating between Tico Tico Tacos and Korean BBQ, he noticed a shiny brass plaque with the name Dr. C. Hasegawa Plastic Surgery.

He entered Dr. Hasegawa's office, where displayed on the office wall were many impressive-looking university diplomas in both English and Japanese. Dino explained to Dr. Hasegawa what his problem was, but did not tell him that he had been rejected by dozens of plastic surgeons.

The following day, Dr. Hasegawa performed a five-hour surgical procedure on Dino's face. When the bandages were removed, Dino looked at himself in the mirror and was shocked, but not disappointed, by what he saw. He thanked Dr. Hasegawa profusely for a job well done. All were happy—he, because he no longer looked like the annoyingly handsome man he never wanted to be, and the doctor, because he had taken a face with quite ordinary occidental features and given it extraordinarily Asian ones.

After the swelling had gone and the bruises healed, Dino dyed his blonde hair black and ventured out into the world. He quickly discovered that plastic surgery was not the solution. The operation had done nothing but add more Asians to his band of adoring women.

Without comprehending why, he often found himself lunching at Sushi Heaven, where he became intrigued with Mika, a demure Japanese waitress who seemed to look at him differently than most women did. So differently that, one day, he asked why she kept staring at him. She apologized profusely and then, being uncharacteristically forward, asked if she might ask him a personal question.

"Shoot!" Dino answered.

"You have very nice black hair, sir," she said with a impish smile, "and I wondered why you dye your roots blond?"

He laughed and told Mika his life's story and about the curse of being so handsome.

"I don't think you're so handsome," she said softly.

"You don't?" he asked suspiciously. "You're not just saying that?"

"No," she said, looking into his eyes, "but you seem to be a very sensitive person."

Dino spent the rest of the day driving his truck at half-speed and thinking about dear, sweet-faced Mika. Did she really think he was not that handsome?

That evening Dino returned to Sushi Heaven and ate two dinners while waiting for Mika to finish work.

At ten o'clock, over a cup of green tea, Dino told Mika, "I like you a lot," adding, "Since I told you about myself, I think it's only fair that you tell me about yourself."

At midnight, when the restaurant closed, Dino offered to drive Mika home. He thought of calling a cab, but decided that she liked him well enough to ride in his two-ton beer truck.

"A beer truck?" she screeched, "You're taking me home in a beer truck?"

"I just thought," he said apologetically, "that it'd be fun for you."

"Fun??" she squealed.

"Well, I thought—"

"I'm so excited. In Japan my father drove a truck. The best memories I have are of him driving me to school in his big Sapporo beer truck."

After saying goodnight to Mika, Dino said again, "I like you, a lot," this time adding, "...a whole lot!!!"

G.G. Giggler

"John, why in heaven's name did you bring that girl here?"

"Don't you remember, sis? It was you, Prissy, who suggested I bring a date so you can keep your boy-girl dinner seating arrangement intact."

"I meant an appropriate date. You couldn't consider Gigi an appropriate date."

"Not Gigi. G.G.," John explained, "she uses her initials."

"Does Miss Initials have a name?"

"Yes, Ginny Giggler."

"Giggler??"

"Her Polish grandfather shortened their name from Gigglerkowski to Giggler."

"Well, her name's appropriate. John, does she ever stop giggling?"

"I hope not. I enjoy her giggle, it's melodic."

"It's annoying."

"Prissy! G.G. is a happy person."

"Or blissfully ignorant."

"You always find happy people annoying. Sis, you should look into that."

"What is she so happy about, her height?"

"And her hair, teeth, and legs... or didn't you notice that she has an astounding figure?"

"I noticed how parts of her jiggles when she giggles. John, you've got to get that Amazon out of here before Dad arrives."

"I can't do that. I promised G.G. that she would finally get to meet Dad."

"What do you mean, 'Finally get to meet Dad?' How long have you known the giggler?"

"About two months, but I didn't get to know what an extraordinary person she is until she moved in with me."

"Are you serious?"

"Deadly. I've asked her to marry me."

"No!"

"We've set the time and place, Atlantic City, the day after her appearance in the Miss America Pageant."

"John, please tell me this is one of your practical jokes."

"No joke, sis, I love her."

Prissy was hoping to see her brother's face break into a smile and say, 'Just kidding, sis,' but no smile broke.

'That bastard,' she thought, 'is going to change the raison d'etre of my dinner party. My Welcome-Back-From-The-Dead-Daddy-Celebration will become a Welcome-To-The-Family-G.G.-Disaster. Instead of Daddy discussing his remarkable recovery from a heart attack, we'll be hearing about Miss Giggler's dream of becoming Miss Friggin' America!'

Prissy's hopes for salvaging her party were dealt a blow when she heard the front door open and her father, Kirk J. Kingsley, ask,

"And who might you be, young lady?"

Two short giggles bracketed her response, "I'm G.G., John's friend."

Her father saying, "Well, I am Kirk Kingsley, John's Dad, and aren't you pretty," was Prissy's cue to step in and stop any further bonding between them. Prissy was slowed by the clusters of guests who insisted on telling her how beautiful she looked and how grateful they were to be at the party. Prissy had invited a mix of honest and dishonest gushers, all of whom owed her father, Kirk J. Kingsley, money, homage and their livelihood.

"Prissy, my dear," Kirk sang, greeting his daughter with a peck on the cheek, "what do you think of our Miss Giggler?"

"Our Miss Giggler, Dad?" Prissy asked, What do you mean, our Miss Giggler?"

"It's all right, darling, I know all about it. John called me last night and spilled the beans."

"What beans are those?" Prissy asked.

"Prissy dear, I know how you planned for this to be a surprise party, but your brother worried that my heart got all the shocks it could take from those damned defibrillator paddles. I want to thank you for arranging this engagement party for your brother and his fiancée.

"Did you know that this lovely future sister-in-law of yours is going to be in the Miss America pageant?"

"Yes, and isn't it wonderful?" Prissy lied, taking G.G.'s arm. "And I think she's going to win. I can't imagine anyone at the pageant being more beautiful, can you, John?"

"Well, no," her brother said, smiling and kissing his fiancée's hand, "but beauty is not the only thing the contestants are judged on. Talent and intelligence are at least as important, and believe me, G.G. is no slouch in either of those departments."

Hearing G.G. giggle too long and too loudly at her brother's pronouncement made Prissy realize what she had to do:

Expose her future sister-in-law's shortcomings by making her the focus of attention. Not only would it keep her company entertained, but it might stop her brother from destroying his life. She would become Jane Pauley and Miss Giggler would be her sole guest.

The one-on-one interview started as they sat down to dinner.

"Sooooo, G.G., dear," Prissy began, "Tell us about yourself. Where are you from?"

"Well," G.G. giggled, "it's a funny story and most people laugh when I tell it."

"Oh, tell us, dear." Prissy prompted. "We can all use a good laugh."

"Well, I was born in Walla Walla," she giggled, "where they grow those sweet onions? Now, this may sound like I'm making it up, but when I was six, my father, who works for the Coca-Cola company, was transferred from Walla Walla to Maui, where, can you believe it, they grow even sweeter onions?"

The dinner guests managed forced smiles, but Prissy was unhappy to note that her father was beaming from ear to ear.

"So how was it?" Prissy asked, feigning interest. "Was it fun?"

"Well," G.G. said, starting a new series of giggles, "as my mother always says, 'We didn't stay there long enough to get a tan.' Daddy was called back to Atlanta and assigned to... now, where do you think?" She stopped giggling long enough to say, "Vidalia, Georgia, where they grow the sweetest onions of all!"

"Well, isn't that interesting?" Prissy gushed.

"It is interesting, isn't it?! And," G.G. giggled, "it gets way more interesting."

"I don't see how it can. Tell us more," Prissy prodded.

"Well, while we were living in Georgia," G.G. offered demurely, "I entered my very first beauty contest and I won. Guess what I was crowned?"

"Miss Onion?" Prissy asked amiably.

"No, Miss Sweet Onion, but you were close," she whooped. "John, you told your sister about me being Miss Sweet Onion, didn't you?"

"I did not, honey."

"John, you're joshing," G.G. giggled, turning to Prissy. "Your brother told you, didn't he?"

"No, he didn't," Prissy said, kissing her pinkie to God, "I swear!"

G.G. smiled and starting, sniffing the air, "Now who's responsible for the wonderful onion soup I'm smelling?"

"How did you know?" Prissy asked. "The kitchen door is closed. Does anyone else smell the soup?"

All shook their heads.

"Another one of G.G.'s talents that I didn't know she had," John said, proudly patting her shoulder.

"You ought to add it to your Miss America talent resume," Prissy offered as the butler entered carrying a silver tureen. "Those extra points might be the margin of victory."

"It is so amazing," giggled G.G., ignoring Prissy's sarcasm, "that you would be serving me onion soup when I was telling you how onions have been such a big part of my life. Prissy, I am so happy you made this soup. It'll make my onion story more interesting next time I tell it."

A contented Prissy smiled sweetly as she listened to G.G. giggling and rattling on about onions and onion soup. Ginny Giggler was having the desired negative effect on their guests and, more importantly, on John. During the soup course, Prissy decided to go in for the kill.

"You know, G.G., I have seen every Miss America pageant in the last ten years," Prissy offered, "and do you know what I've noticed?"

"What, Prissy? But, before you tell me I have to say a word about this onion soup. I swear, it is the best I have ever eaten. Now, if you don't want to share your kitchen secrets, I'd understand, but if you do, I'd love to have your recipe for it."

"And you shall," Prissy said sweetly. "I'll write it out for you."

"Oh, thank you. Now when I tell my onion story," she giggled, "I can add that Prissy Kingsley gave me the recipe for the world's most delicious French onion soup."

Prissy was thrilled with the reception G.G.'s stories were getting. All of her guests' eyebrows were raised, and the few who weren't eating had their mouths open. John was aware of what his sister was doing, but had faith that by evening's end everyone would love and respect G.G. as he did.

"Prissy," G.G. said, remembering, "you said that you noticed something about the pageant?"

"Oh, yes," Prissy happily recalled, "I noticed in the last few years that the girls who won were not always the prettiest but were the ones who gave the best and most sincere answers to the master of ceremonies' questions."

"Yes, that's true," G.G. agreed innocently.

"Well," Prissy continued, "I wondered if you've given much thought to how you might answer those questions."

"Oh, I have," she giggled. "We're not told what the questions will be, but that's the challenge. I think I'll be ready for whatever they ask. You know what might be fun," she said, giggling a short giggle. "I hope I'm not monopolizing your dinner."

A chorus of sarcastic "Oh nos" and "Not at alls" and "Don't be sillys" were misread by G.G. and gave her leave to suggest that it might be fun if she answered questions that Prissy or any of her guests cared to ask.

"It would be ever so helpful," G.G. pleaded. "Would you mind?"

"Not at all," Prissy offered. "If you become Miss America, we can say we helped. Ready?"

"I am ready!"

"G.G., darling," John angrily interjected, "do you think this is a good idea?"

"I do," G.G. insisted. "Fire away, Prissy!"

"Miss Sweet Onion, if you—"

"Miss Georgia!" G.G. corrected.

"Sorry! Uh, Miss Georgia, if you were to become Miss America, how would you use your power to improve mankind?"

G.G. sat up straight in her chair, squared her shoulders, and took a deep breath. She was the only one in the room who seemed unaware that these posture adjustments called attention to her perfectly proportioned bosom. Poised and confident, G.G. closed her eyes and took the time she needed to formulate her answer.

Prissy expected her response to contain many giggled inanities. "If I were to become Miss America," G.G. began, in a well-modulated contralto voice, "I would do everything in my power to save human lives. If, in my lifetime, I am able to save one life, I will consider it a life well spent."

No one at the table seemed to care that she was speaking in platitudes. They had expected as much, but no one had imagined that she could say whole sentences without giggling. That surprised even her fiancé, who had never before heard her speak in this low, serious voice. Kirk Kingsley was quite aware of the nasty little game his daughter was playing.

Prissy's displeasure with her brother's choice of mate was apparent, but so was her beauty. Kirk Kingsley popped a piece of warm sourdough bread into his mouth and thought seriously about using Miss Georgia as a spokesperson for "PLEASSSURE," the international cosmetics firm he had recently acquired.

Disappointed that her pigeon was able to suppress her giggle, Prissy gambled that Miss Sweet Onion could not suppress her stupidity.

"Tell us, Miss Georgia," Prissy asked "when you say your goal is to save lives, how exactly would you do this?"

"Well, G.G." stated simply, "as a doctor, I'd advocate our Congress vote for bills that would outlaw guns, wars, pollution, poverty, electric chairs, lethal injections and nuclear weapons... and things like that."

Encouraged by the guests' stifled laughter, and her father's reaction, Prissy pressed on.

"Miss Georgia, when you said 'save lives as a doctor,' are we to assume that you intend to study medicine?"

"I do, and hopefully by next semester, if I cut down on my volunteer work at the AIDS clinic and the senior citizens' hospices, which I would not like to do, I will register for college."

As she was asking it, Prissy wondered whether she would regret quipping, "G.G., do you ever make time to go to the toilet?"

This flippancy gave everyone who had been stifling laughter permission to explode, and explode they did. Prissy was stunned by the reaction, and proud that she had succeeded in amusing her guests while ridiculing her brother's fiancée. One of the guests, who had a high-pitched cackle, became the catalyst for the more repressed ridiculers, who, feeding off the cackler and each other, including Kirk Kingsley, were soon holding their sides, wiping tears from their eyes and asking each other to, "Stop, stop, stop!"

G.G., who had every right to feel mortified and angry, was deathly calm and stared straight ahead. John tried to put his arm around her, but she pushed his arm aside defiantly and walked away. John dashed after her, almost knocking her over when she stopped short at the head of the table, where John's Dad was seated. G.G. had seen him flailing his arms and making strange, choking sounds... something was lodged in his esophagus. The laughter cut off abruptly when G.G. shouted to everyone, "Mr. Kingsley is choking! Is there a doctor in the house?"

"I invited his doctor, but he couldn't make it," a devastated and guilt-ridden Prissy said. "Can't we do something?"

"We can try a Heimlich maneuver, which I can do, but with his heart condition... I don't know."

Without waiting for an opinion or permission or physical help from either of his children, G.G. lifted the 190-pound tycoon out of his chair, placed her fist under his rib cage, and deftly applied the Heimlich maneuver. The old man coughed up a small piece of sourdough bread and managed a smile before fainting. G.G. diagnosed that he suffered from oxygen deprivation and ordered John to fetch the oxygen canister that she assumed would be in his bedroom.

On September 18, 1999, Kirk J. Kingsley and all the business and blood members of his family drove in a motorcade of stretch limousines to Atlantic City's convention hall, where they rooted noisily for Miss Georgia to win the big prize. After watching G.G. Giggler graciously acknowledge the thunderous applause and the standing ovation she received for her flawless piano rendition of Gershwin's Concerto in F, a happy but conflicted John convinced himself that there were worse things in life than having to wait a year before marrying Miss America, who, in four years, would get a medical degree in endocrinology.

Deibenquist Sounds Famous

"So, Scoop darling, what do you think?"

"I like it, Ceil, I really do. It's easy on the eyes and it's modern, just like you described it. It's a very pleasant painting, very pleasant."

"Isn't it? I think it will fit perfectly with the color scheme I'm planning for the dining room."

"And the price isn't out of line, considering the prices they're getting for paintings these days."

"Whorley Deibenquist. Is he very famous?"

"Well, I don't know about 'very' famous but he must be famous enough. No one asks for thirty thousand dollars for a painting unless they're some kind of famous. You know, I think I've heard of him, Whorley Deibenquist! He sounds famous."

"Like Pablo Picasso?"

"Nobody is as famous as Pablo Picasso, hon. Pablo got fifty-four 'mill' for one of his jobs. No, this Deibenquist isn't in the same league with Pablo."

"How do we know this guy's any good?"

"The price, Ceil. The price tells you how good anyone is. Would Floyd Mayweather or Manny Pacquiao get thirty million dollars for a fight if they weren't any good?"

"They weren't very good in their last fight."

"Good enough so that nobody asked for their money back."

"If this artist is so good, why is the painting only thirty thousand?"

"That's because he's young. I'll bet when Picasso was his age he wasn't getting any thirty thou a painting. He was lucky to get thirty pesos. I say we buy it."

"Really?"

"Of course really. Isn't that why you had me look at it?"

"You're right, but maybe we can offer him eighteen thousand... tell him I'm a decorator."

"But you're not."

"I have my cousin's resale number."

"Ceil, you don't bargain for great art."

"How do we know it's great art?"

"Well, for one thing, he's painted the trees so they don't look exactly like trees but you can tell that they are."

"That's true. How about the painting we saw at Sheila's friend's studio? That sky had a very similar soft, pink color that I want to use for the walls. It was much larger than this one and she only wanted eight hundred dollars for it."

"Honey, we got a custom-built home. Do you want to cock it up with an eight hundred dollar piece of art that was painted by your cousin Sheila's girlfriend... what's her name?"

"You're right, darling. We don't even know her name. Oh, I hope this one fits in with my decor. I'm only guessing that the colors will match."

"You got a good eye, Ceil. You found those great tangerine throw pillows that match the walls of my waiting room. I don't know how you did that."

"Well, I did cheat a little, Scoop. I took a tangerine with me when I went looking for those pillows. I wish I had brought a paint sample with me. I don't know, darling, I'm so undecided about this Deibenquest painting."

"Deiben*quist*."

"What?"

"You said Deibenquest. It's Deibenquist."

"Well, I wish Mr. Deiben*quist* had painted in some more birds in flight. I wonder if he would."

"I don't think so, honey. The painting is called '*Bird in Flight*.'"

"He could change it to 'Birds in Flight.' That's easy to do."

"I know, pumpkin, but you can't ask an artist to paint in extra birds if he don't feel they belong."

"But the bird is the perfect powder blue I need. It would help so much if it were a bigger bird. Could we ask him to make the bird bigger?"

"No, artists don't work that way."

"Suppose you tell him he has a definite sale if he adds a couple more birds."

"Ceil, with a real artist it's a take-it-or-leave-it proposition, that much I know."

"You're probably right. I like the painting. I know it won't clash with our floral dinnerware and the color of the bird is a perfect match for the seat cushions. I just wish the bird was a little bigger..."

"I trust your eyes, Ceil. Here's how I look at it. The colors aren't a perfect match, but if you can live with the painting for a year, I'll put it up for auction. If the gallery owner wasn't handing me a load of bull manure about this Deibenquist guy, my guesstimate is that we'll end up with a couple of thou profit."

Both Ceil and Scoop guessed wrong. The colors were way off (the sky was many shades lighter than Ceil's walls and the small blue bird did not match her seat cushions). Ceil suffered with her mistake for a year before insisting that Scoop sell "the damn thing." Scoop's guesstimate of a couple thousand dollar profit was even further off. The painting for which they paid eighteen thousand dollars, they sold at auction for one hundred and eighty thousand dollars, giving them a huge profit. Ceil used eight hundred of it to buy a seascape from Sheila's friend who, for an extra hundred, painted in an flock of blue seagulls.

How Paul Robeson
Saved My Life

I was aware that the master sergeant who was urinating beside me was a Negro and I tried to behave as if it was the most natural thing in the world. It wasn't. It was 1943, and the United States Army was just starting to consider treating all men equally. The only integrated barracks at Camp Crowder, Missouri, was the one that housed the training school for non commissioned officers. Being a corporal, I barely qualified as a noncommissioned officer. I wanted so badly for the black man to know how pleased I was that we were in an integrated latrine standing shoulder to shoulder and proudly pissing for our country. A few moments later, once again side by side, we washed our hands. I ventured a "Hi" and got a "Hi" back. We started a conversation that began with, "What outfit are you with?" and ended five minutes later with our having mutual knowledge of each other's hometown, schooling, marital status and favorite jazz singers.

I was aware that at the far end of the latrine a blond crew cut tech sergeant stood urinating and observing us engaging in social intercourse. He kept glaring at me as he buttoned his fly. I thought we must have upset him, or why would he leave before washing his hands?

The master sergeant and I shook hands and wished each other luck surviving the war. He climbed to the second floor of the barracks where the "colored" noncoms were assigned and I went to my bunk on the first floor, where I found the blond crew-cut sergeant sitting on my footlocker.

"Staff Sergeant Andrew 'Bull' Warington," he said, extending his unwashed hand. "Corporal Carl Reiner," I shot back, reluctantly taking his hand.

I gave him a wet fish-like handshake instead of my normal manly one and immediately regretted it, for I had now advertised myself as Jewish sissy, while risking an infection. I started to ask him where he hailed from, but he interrupted me to ask if I didn't think it was "a fuckin' shame" that we had to live with "the damn niggers." My hesitation was all the answer he needed.

"Corporal," he said, squinting at me, "are you saying you don't mind living with niggers?"

"They're not really living with us, they're living *above us*."

174

I wondered if the sergeant noticed that I referred to our black brethren as "they" instead of "niggers." I was considering saying Negroes, which was the choice of most non-racists back then, but I chickened out. Visions of the Ku Klux Klan were dancing in my head.

"It don't bother you, Corporal, that they're puttin' their black asses on our toilet seats and they're usin' our fuckin' showers? That don't bother you damn Yankees?"

Being born of Austrian-Romanian parents, I had never thought of myself as a damn Yankee. I was flattered. I told the sergeant as politely as I could that it didn't bother me that they were sharing the latrine, unless they pissed on the toilet seats or shat in the shower.

I'd be annoyed, I added, if anyone did that, present company included.

A few of the noncoms chuckled, and I suspected among them I had an ally or two.

"Are you sayin' that you think a fuckin' nigger is as good as a white man?" Sergeant Warington asked bluntly.

We were now back in the eleventh century, he the inquisitor, and I the heretic, but how to tell His Holiness that he was full of shit without putting myself in danger of being lynched.

"You asked," I said, annunciating each word with a quasi-Shakespearian delivery, "if I considered that a fucking nigger was as good as a fucking white man?" I rubbed my chin thoughtfully and said, "I honestly don't know. That Sergeant Williams seemed like a nice guy."

"You tellin' me that that fuckin' nigger is as good as you?!"

"Probably better," I suggested, "I know he's a lot better educated than I am, and in hand-to-hand combat I bet he can beat the shit out of both of us."

I wondered that I had gone too far, but a few noncoms laughed out loud and I relaxed. I have found my strategy! Laughs! I will go for laughs! When I heard the snap in his voice, I knew the battle was joined.

"You sayin', Corporal, that a nigger can be as good as a white man?"

"I was saying, Sergeant, that it is within the realm of possibility that a *particular* nigger could, in some ways, be as good or even superior to a *particular* white man."

"And I'm tellin' you, Corporal," the sergeant explained, as if I was a school child who had missed a lesson, "there is no fuckin' nigger in this world as good as me, and there is no fuckin' black ass cook superior to me."

"Somewhere in this vast world, Sergeant," I dared to suggest, "there may be some niggers who are your equal."

"Name one!" he challenged.

I laughed and told him we were engaging in a silly exercise. He responded by placing his nose against mine.

"If you can name one," he shouted into my mouth, "I'll kiss your big white ass."

"I accept the challenge," I explained, "and if by some remote chance I win, I'd rather you kiss someone else's ass... any volunteers?"

The boys hooted and hollered and some raised their hands.

"CORPORAL," he screamed, "NAME A NIGGER! THAT'S AN ORDER."

"PAUL ROBESON, SIR!" I answered smartly.

"Alright, you tell me what that nigger, Paul Robeson, has done and I'll match him nine ways to January."

I suggested we were engaging in a pointless exercise, and he accused me of bluffing and trying to back out of the challenge. When he put his nose up against mine again and insisted I tell him, 'one fuckin' thing the nigger has done,' I informed him that Paul Robeson had graduated Phi Beta Kappa from Rutgers University.

"I never went to college," the sergeant countered proudly.

One of the noncoms found this amusing and I quickly chose him to be our scorekeeper.

"Put down one for the sarge and one for Robeson. So far we're even."

I then offered that Paul Robeson spoke twenty languages, in twelve of which he was fluent or near fluent.

"Spoke twelve foreign languages, eh?" he said emphatically. "Well, I speak *American.*"

'Two to two,' I shouted to my scorekeeper, who laughed and held up two fingers on each hand.

Spurred on by an audience whose responses were heartening, I began to enjoy myself.

The following is a remembered transcript of the historic debate.

Me: "Paul Robeson was a four-letter man at his college and was voted an All-American in football."

Sarge: "I never went to college, and before I enlisted I managed a grocery market." (*chuckles from the group*)

Me: "Three to three, still even. Paul Robeson has written books."

Sarge: (*smirking*) "I never read a book."

Me: "Four to four. Damn! I thought I had you on that one." (*good healthy response from the guys*)

Me: "Paul Robeson has a degree in law."

Sarge: "My daddy is a lawyer and has an office in downtown New Orleans."

Me: "Got me again, dammit. Five to five. Paul Robeson is an actor and a singer and has appeared in concert, on Broadway and in motion pictures."

177

Sarge: "And I am (*here he paused for effect*) a Louisiana state board-certified embalmer and I have worked as a chief embalmer in the biggest mortuary in Shreveport."

On hearing this, I threw my hands up and conceded defeat. I congratulated him on the brilliance of his strategy, playing possum, and waiting for just the right moment to drop the bomb. I admitted that if Paul Robeson was called upon to embalm a finger, much less a whole corpse, he would be at a loss. I then patted the sergeant on the back, grinned, and good-naturedly called him a sonofabitch for booby-trapping me the way he did. He cocked his head and wondered if he was being complimented or ridiculed. The Sarge concluded from the laughter and chatter that he was being derided. He moved toward me with clench fists and I fully expected to be punched in the face. Instead, he brushed past me, smiling in that strange way that villains do when they lose a round to the hero and leave. You know they will return.

That evening, the Sarge and I passed each other in the mess hall. I forced a smile and he responded with a sneer that seemed to say, "I'm not finished with you!"

At nine o'clock that night, I climbed into my upper bunk, laid my head on my pillow and waited for the other shoe to drop. It was lights-out and the barracks were ominously quiet, or so it seemed to me. The soldiers who were not burdened with neurotic guilt and fear were sound asleep before the bugler's last note had faded, and then it came! From across the room a voice with a gentle southern drawl drifted toward me, "Corporal Reiner, you awake?"

"Yes, Sergeant?" I whispered back.

"What say you and me step outside with our carbines?"

"Huh?" I asked, hiding my fear.

"I think, Corporal," he continued, sweetly addressing me as if he was at a cotillion and was asking me for a dance, "if you and me went into the field with our carbines we'd find out once and for all which one of us is right about the damn niggers. It'd be fun, don't ya think?"

"Yes, Sarge, it could be fun," I said blithely, "but I'm not about to go to jail for life just for a little fun."

I now had the attention of a barrack full of chuckling witnesses.

"I am a first-class marksman," I lied, "with three medals to prove it. If we faced off with carbines, I'd probably blow your head off while your finger was still searching for the trigger. Sarge, I'm not about to screw up my life over an argument over racial superiority when you've already won the damn debate."

The men, who had remained noncommittal during the sergeant's invitation to a dual, now erupted with a melange of laughter, cat calls, a reminder that it was way past lights-out, and a suggestion that we "shut the fuck up!"

Within seconds, there was a stony silence that I did not expect would last. I knew the sergeant would want the last word and that word turned out to be my name, Reiner.

"Ryyyyyyyyynuh," he sang, elongating the first syllable to the breaking point and continued with, "Yyyyew a Jyyyew?"

I admitted I was Jewish and asked why he asked.

With a voice that seemed to brim with nostalgia, the sergeant informed me that one of his best friends back home was a "Jyyyew."

"Ben Goldfarb?" he asked expectantly, thinking I would know him because we were both Jewish.

My adrenalin flow was slowed and all I could think to say was, "Ben Goldfarb? No, I don't think I know him."

Those were the last words Sergeant Andrew 'Bull' Warington and I exchanged. About a year later, I learned that the sergeant had been wounded and received a medical discharge. Some time after that a non-com who was present at the historic Robeson debate showed me a clipping from the camp paper of the sergeant going back to his home in Louisiana and being elected to a seat in the legislature. It did not spell out whether it was a state or federal seat, so I did not know whether to be concerned for the future of his state or the future of our country.

Aunt Delia
& Her Twins

ORRIN TUTTLE felt confident that today was going to be a pro-ductive one. It was quickly confirmed when he saw a Federal Express van pull away from the curb and leave a parking space directly in front of the building where his new job interview was to take place. With a minimum amount of jockeying, he eased his BMW into the space.

'Now,' he thought, *'if I could just slip into this job as smoothly.'*

He sprang from the car, strode to the parking meter, and extracted four coins from his pockets, three nickels and a penny!

"Dammit!" he mumbled, loudly enough to startle an elderly gentlewoman.

"Damn what?" she asked, turning to him.

"I'm sorry," he explained, "I don't have quarters for the parking meter, and I have an important appointment in a few minutes. You wouldn't have change for a twenty-dollar bill, would you?"

"I think I do, young man," she said, opening her purse while scanning Orrin's face. "If I'm not being too forward, may I ask your name?"

"Orrin Tuttle. Why do you ask?"

"It's uncanny, but you're the spitting image of my nephew Larry."

"That's interesting. Uh, do you have the change?"

"I'm sure I do," she said, opening her wallet, "Oh, I'm so sorry, but it seems all I have are twenties and fifties; but there's a newsstand at the corner. I'm sure Jimmy will oblige you, he's very nice. I'll go with you. I know you're in a hurry but I won't hold you up. I'm a very brisk walker, even though I'll be seventy-nine next Thursday. By the way, my name is Delia."

"How do you do, Delia?" he mumbled as he tried to pull away.

"As you can see, I do very well." she shouted, quickening her pace. "Actually, it's Cordelia, Cordelia West. My father was Jonathan West of West Industries."

"Oh yes. Well, it was nice to...," he mumbled incoherently, hoping to end their relationship.

"We Wests are a hearty lot," she persisted. "Daddy lived to be ninety-nine but Uncles Franklin and Theodore, who made their home in California, passed on at eighty-five and eighty-eight. The West Coast Wests didn't fare as well as the East Coast Wests." She laughed at the little family joke.

The two arrived at the newsstand in a dead heat. While Orrin was trying to catch his breath, Delia negotiated with the newsstand dealer.

"Captain Jimmy, this gentleman needs change for a twenty-dollar bill. I'll vouch for the fact that it's a twenty!"

"Because Jimmy is blind," Delia explained, walking back to the car, "he is reluctant to make change for strangers."

Orrin put the quarters in the meter, thanked Delia sincerely for helping him, and apologized for seeming curt.

"Young man, I appreciate your sensitivity. Most young people today have little patience for older folk."

"Well," Orrin offered, "back in Gadsden, Alabama, we learned to respect our elders or else."

Orrin started for the building and got as far as the revolving door when he heard her call his name.

"Orrin, what kind of a job are you looking for?"

He knew he had to answer or risk being followed into the building.

"I'm being interviewed for an account executive position in an advertising firm."

"I don't believe it," she said, clapping her gloved hands together.

"I beg your pardon?"

"Is Tuttle your real name or are you by any chance adopted?"

If Delia had asked any other question than that he might have wished her a "Good day" and bolted for the elevator.

"Mrs. West," he said, smiling, "that's a very unusual question to ask a stranger."

"Oh, I'm aware of that. Were you adopted?"

"I must know why you asked me that."

"Well, Orrin, my nephew Larry West, who I said could be your twin, is not my natural nephew. My youngest brother, Sebastian, and his wife, Ardelle, were not able to have children... medical problems that they never shared with me. In any event, they adopted this darling little baby, Larry, who so reminds me of you. Your hair color, the blue-green eyes, the height, the way you carry yourself, even your way of speaking. I hope you don't think I'm an addled old woman, but I assure you I have never walked up to another person and said I thought you were my nephew's twin, but good god, I think you are. Are you adopted?"

Orrin checked his watch and realized that in five minutes he would be late for his interview. He took Delia by the arm and led her into the building. He found a quiet corner in the marble lobby and explained to her it was a big joke in his family. "I was constantly chided about being adopted. As you can see, I am blond, and six feet, three inches tall and my parents are both brunette and five foot three inches tall."

"Did you ever ask them if you are adopted?"

"Oh, sure, when I was fifteen-years-old and towered above them they laughed and swore I was their natural child and I should never doubt it."

"Well, if you met my nephew Larry, you might."

"Your nephew knows he's adopted?"

"Oh, yes, but he doesn't know who his natural parents are. He's very eager to find them, and I must say that Sebastian and Ardele are very supportive of his desire to do so. They have given him all the information they have, and so far it has led nowhere. Did I mention that Larry is in advertising?"

"No, you didn't."

"He's the director of the commercial art department at Bigelow & Smutz."

"Oh my god, I used to work for Bigelow & Smutz... my first job."

"I know."

"How could you?"

"When Larry started there last Fall, an old maintenance man told Larry how there was a tall, blond man who used to work there who looked a lot like him. It had to be you."

"Mrs. West," Orrin asked, inhaling deeply, "could you arrange for us to meet?"

Orrin's head was spinning. He handed Delia a business card and told her to call him later that day. Cordelia West found herself smiling as she watched the dazed young man walk slowly toward the elevators.

During the interview with Samuel Simmons of Simmons, Paltrow & Scott, Orrin kept imagining himself as a twin. He was plainly distracted, but somehow managed to keep enough of his personality intact to impress Mr. Simmons. The job was his if he wanted it.

When Orrin arrived home, on his answering machine he heard, "Orrin, this is your Aunt Delia. I know I'm being premature calling myself your aunt, but Larry is coming to dinner tonight and I'm hoping you'll join us."

Orrin jotted down the address and time, and then considered his options. He realized he had none. He had to see this Larry and find out if his folks had lied to him.

Orrin found it difficult deciding what to wear for this occasion. "Hey Tuttle," he addressed himself in the mirror, "you're not going to a wedding, you're going to meet someone who may look like you..."

He opted for the outfit he had worn all day. If it was good enough to land a high-paying job, it was good enough for this weird dinner date.

Knowing the parking problems on Fifth Avenue and Seventy-eight Street, Orrin chose to leave himself a cushion of time. Since today seemed to be his day, he was not surprised to find a spot just two car lengths from the canopied entrance to Delia's apartment building. As Orrin approached the entrance, the red-uniformed doorman tipped his hat.

"Evening, Mr. Tuttle," he said, opening the ornate brass door. "You do look like Mrs. West's nephew Larry," he explained, reading the puzzled look on Orrin's face. "She said to go right up."

Orrin smiled and allowed himself to be ushered through the lobby and into the elevator.

"Orrin!" Delia sang out as her butler opened the door. "I'm so glad you came early. Larry did too. He can't wait to meet you. I reached him at his girlfriend's home in East Hampton and he helicoptered in this morning."

Delia took Orrin by the hand and led him down a long hall. She informed him that his "twin" was in the library, eagerly awaiting their rendezvous. When they entered, Larry was in the process of pouring a vintage Pinot Noir into a wine-glass.

"Larry, darling," Delia gushed, "I want you to meet Orrin Tuttle, and Orrin, this is my favorite nephew, Larry West."

They mumbled inaudible hellos and exchanged firm handshakes. All three members of the summit meeting stood silently for a long moment, Orrin and Larry studying each other and Delia studying them both.

"It's absolutely uncanny, how much you look alike. Don't you feel as if you are looking into a mirror?"

They turned slowly to look at Delia.

"Oh, gracious," she shouted, "I've read how twins, even if separated at birth, will do things like that."

"Like what?" Larry asked.

"Like you and Orrin just did, turning to look at me at exactly the same time."

"Aunt Delia, you asked us a question and we naturally turned to you."

"Yes, but at precisely the same moment and with precisely the same expression on your faces."

Larry and Orrin turned to each other and smiled.

"There!" Delia pointed out. "You did it again, same head turn, same smile and now you are shaking your head the same way. Twins do that. I know I'm right about you two!"

"Aunt Delia," Larry demurred, "as much as you seem to want us to be twins, I don't think Orrin and I are."

"I have to agree with Larry," Orrin said. "Oh, there is a sort of resemblance, but not as you described."

Delia collapsed into an easy chair and shook her head sadly. "I was so sure you looked like twins. I must be getting senile."

"Aunt Delia, if I can be honest, your problem is not senility, it's vanity. If you would just put on your glasses, you would see what *is* and not what you wish things to be."

"Oh, I guess you're right, as always, Larry," Delia sighed, picking up a crystal dinner bell and shaking it vigorously. "Why don't we make the best of my silly little farrago and enjoy the rest of the evening? I've had our cook prepare us a lovely dinner. Your favorite, Larry, Poulet Vinaigre."

"Vinegar chicken!" Orrin said, his voice rising half an octave, "I love vinegar chicken!"

"Are you saying that to be a good guest?" Larry asked, smiling.

"No. My college roommate's mother was French, she made it every time I asked."

"Well, there you are," snapped Delia. "I knew there was something about you two!"

"Orrin, perhaps we are related. Maybe first cousins."

"I'd say more likely second cousins," Orrin countered, staring at Larry's face.

"Yes," Larry answered, putting his hand on Orrin's chin and turning his face to see his profile, "second cousins twice removed."

Delia was happy to hear her dinner guests laugh and continue to conjecture about how distant their relationship might be.

Orrin and Larry, related or not, had a good deal more in common than many blood relatives have. At dinner, they touched on many diverse subjects and found they held similar views.

On things political and social, they were in total agreement.

Later, over coffee in the den, they traded observations and opinions about the people in the world of advertising whom they both knew. Again, they were in accord as to who were and were not "horses' asses."

From a vantage point across the room, Delia watched with pride as her nephew and her abductee enjoyed their cigars and each other's company.

The following day, Larry introduced Orrin to his best-friend, Sondra, who found Orrin to be delightful and endearing as he described.

At their wedding ceremony on the flowered back lawn of Aunt Delia's estate in South Hampton, Sondra was both happy and sad. Sad that the dynamics of her long friendship with Larry would be changing, but happy that Larry had chosen her to act as his best person at his and Orrin's wedding.

Delia felt something very special, and allowed herself to weep openly as she accepted dozens of congratulations at her brilliant match making. Among the well wishers were her brother and sister-in-law, the beaming Mr. and Mrs. Sebastian West, who adored their son Larry's choice of mate, and the less pleased Republican congressman Wilber Harte Tuttle who, only a week earlier, had learned about his son Orrin's sexual orientation.

Three months after the ceremony, as a belated wedding present to his son and son-in-law, Congressman Tuttle, with some prodding from his wife, voted aye on Prop 8, the comprehensive gay rights amendment.

As Easy as ABC

In 1987, Leo Fromm's radio alarm clicked on and blared out the last six bars of the *Eroica* Symphony. Leo was jolted awake and sat bolt upright in his bed. Without checking the time, he started to put on the same underwear, socks, jeans, and flannel work shirt he had worn the day before. He could not afford to lose a minute of valuable time searching his room for fresher clothes, if indeed there were any. Leo had had a particularly bad Sunday, and he knew that he would have to work that much harder today. Things were getting out of hand and he vowed that this Monday he would turn them around. This was the fourth weekend in a row he had committed to his work. He brushed his teeth with a dry brush, then sucked a mouthful of water from the faucet, trying unsuccessfully to rinse away his morning mouth odor. He shoved a couple of pencil stubs into his pocket, grabbed a work composition workbook from under his unmade bed and made his way out of the cluttered apartment.

Leo walked briskly down the four flights of stairs trying to decide where he might be most successful in the day's work. He had worked Times Square all day Friday, Saturday and Sunday without improving his lot one bit. In fact, he had lost ground. He had worked himself into a position where only a miracle could extricate him from a total disaster. Last night, as he'd sat on his bed eating his last chocolate chip cookie, he vowed he would try just one more time.

The new shopping mall might be the answer. It had to be. For a moment, he thought of pretending to be blind and asking a stranger to lead him to the mall. This way, he would not see posters and signs that might get him deeper in trouble, but he decided it would be unfair, it was not the way he played the game. It would be cheating, and he would not be able to face himself if he cheated.

He opened his book, the same classic school workbook, with the black-and-white mottling on the stiff cardboard cover, that he had used in grammar school. The workbook he was poring over now was the one-hundredth one he had bought since leaving school. When he started this project in the fourth grade, he never dreamed that it would be his whole life. He never envisioned the burdensome responsibility he was taking on. He remembered well the words he had written in his workbook. He was seated in the auditorium during a school assembly and happened to glance up at the "Exit" sign.

He jotted down the letters, E X I T, on the back page of his workbook and decided that these letters would have to remain there until he could find an E, an X, an I, and a T to cancel out the original letters. He was thrilled to have invented a game, a diversion he could use to beat the tremendous boredom he tried vainly to fight off in all of his classes. At first he thought it was too simple a game because, within seconds of writing the letters EXIT, he noticed another exit sign to the left of the stage. He quickly crossed out each letter and was even. Staying even was the sole object of the game. He decided it could be great fun, and for awhile it was. He found that the greater the challenge the greater the exhilaration when he met the challenge and won. His first major triumph came in the first week, when he owed himself the letters he collected from a "No Smoking" sign. Within a short time, he found a restaurant named King's Moon. It was perfect. The King in the sign would cancel out the second syllable of Smoking. The S of Smoking and the letters in No would be canceled by the letters in the word Moon.

Had he known what the future of the game held for him, he might have quit, but he couldn't think of quitting now. He made his way to the mall, burying his attention in his notebook, thereby avoiding any signs or posters that would add new letters to his burgeoning list. He already owed himself dozens of letters and punctuation marks, among them the very difficult ones to find, the Q's, the Z's, and the X's. He knew his first priority must be the canceling of the Z's. He rode the elevator to the fourth floor, where he read a new sleep shop had opened. He prayed there would be a mattress ad. He had once seen a potential buyer, "Hour Upon Hour of Happy ZZZZZs." He needed those five Z's. A month earlier he had been badly burnt when passing a parking lot he had seen a fleet of "ZZZZ BEST" Carpet Cleaning trucks. He was tempted to cheat, and having one truck's logo cancel the next ones, but from his angle he saw the whole fleet in a single glance. He had to list all the letters, which included the nettlesome Z's.

He approached the Sleep Shop, drew a deep breath, and looked up. He could not believe his luck. In the window were two mannequins asleep in a king-sized bed. Over each of their heads a cartoon balloon was suspended, with more Z's than he could count. The Z's were in diminishing sizes and the last few were so small that they were barely decipherable. He assumed that even the most minuscule, which was little more than a dot, was a Z and he would use it. He had taken credit for twenty-eight of them and had all but wiped out his Z debt. He felt his heart racing as he crossed off the last of the Z's. He looked up quickly and, with ferret-like glances, he searched the window for more good fortune.

"Omigod," he shrieked as his eyes lit upon the display in the adjoining window: "Queen-Sized Beds and Quilts for the Queenliest Queens in the Queendom." Five Q's! He immediately struck out the five Q's on his list and then, the U's, and all the E's, S's, N's and T's. He filled his lungs with air and found himself smiling for the first time in months. The day had started as he had prayed it would. He needed this kind of bonanza.

For the next day, Leo Fromm went from store to store checking signs, posters and advertisements and managed to cancel out two-thirds of the letters he owed himself. At the Quadraplex Theaters, the marquees took care of another raft of letters.

It was close to nine o'clock when he made his way out of the mall. He had picked up a few new letters, but by and large he had done better than he had in years. If he could keep from picking up any more before he got home he knew, with one more day like today, he would be even. He kept his eyes on his worn Adidas as he raced down the street to the bus stop, trying to avoid seeing candy wrappers and parts of newspapers. His goal, which had eluded him all these years, was to get even, 100 percent even. To have in his book, not one letter or one apostrophe or one period to cross out. Then and only then would he close his book, put it in the closet with the dozens of others, and start living his life, a normal life. He would call his father in Boston and proudly inform him that he would not be needing his monthly allowance anymore. He would call his mother in Miami and tell her he was now ready to work in her gift shop.

He began to fear that he might accidentally pick up some new letters if he kept his eyes open. So, he squinted just enough to blur out the world about him. He half-crossed his eyes as he boarded the bus and found a seat in the back. There he shut his eyes tightly and blocked out everything. Leo Fromm was a tired thirty-five-year-old man who looked seventy.

As the bus snaked its way down the crowded avenue, Leo found himself getting drowsy and, before nodding off, thought of the chocolate chip cookies he had received from his mother. He still had half a tinful, and decided to give himself a party tonight and eat lots of cookies.

"I deserve a party!" he announced loudly.

A few of his fellow passengers looked at him quizzically, but he was oblivious to them as he had fallen asleep. He dreamed that in front of his apartment window a construction crane hoisted a huge billboard that had all the letters and punctuation marks that he owed himself. Then he heard a voice, a deep, hoarse kindly voice, not unlike the pastor in his church.

"My son, thou art troubled. I see it in thy face."

Leo's pastor had never addressed him as "my son," nor did he say "thou" and "thy."

"A heavy weight rests on thy shoulders," the voice continued, "and thou wouldst have that weight lifted. I shall do this for thee, for I am thy savior. Lift up thy head, open wide thine eyes and see the gift I bring thee."

Leo Fromm opened wide his eyes and beheld his bearded savior dressed in a soiled and tattered burlap robe. A crown of thorns fashioned of paper-mache adorned his head. With dirt-encrusted hands, the savior thrust forward a large, grimy cardboard placard.

"Read and be saved!" he bellowed.

Leo began to shake and sob as he read the hand-lettered message that filled every square inch of the placard.

> "Beelzebub, be gone! Be gone, Beelzbub!
> Thou shall not have my soul zealot!
> Beelzebub I exorcise thee zealot!
> Out, Beelzebub! Thou art exorcised!
> Out, Beelzebub! Thou art exorcised!
> Out, Beelzebub! Thou art exorcised!"

Leo was now committed to adding more X's and Z's than he had just stricken from his ledger. He knew he was doomed. He thought of shutting his eyes and forgetting what he'd seen, but his rules didn't allow that. Once he had committed to reading something, he had to enter all the letters. His vision blurred and his lungs started to gasp for air. Into his book Leo hastily scribbled all the accursed Z's and X's.

"Yes, my son," the bearded savior spoke, smiling beatifically at his newest convert, "record these words in your tablet, pass them on to other sinners and thou shalt enter the Kingdom of Heaven. Thou art saved!"

"Thou shalt enter the Kingdom of Heaven," were the last words Leo heard before he got off the bus, keeled over and smashed his head on curb.

———————

Leo entered not the Kingdom of Heaven but the Weisman-Jones Psychiatric Clinic in Poundridge, New York.

Every afternoon, Leo sat placidly under a shady elm tree and stared at his empty hands. Every so often he would look over to where his mother and father were conversing with Dr. Isaac Jones. He could not hear what they were saying, nor did he care. He had more important things on his mind.

Dr. Jones was explaining to Leo's parents that in the four months of therapy Leo had had with his co-director Dr. Weisman, the doctor had achieved a remarkable understanding of their son's letter-matching session, and had managed to dissuade him from asking for pads and pencils.

"I am certain," the doctor explained, "that Leo's silence is only temporary, and we are looking for a complete recovery. What you must decide in these next weeks is whether he goes to Boston with you, Mr. Fromm, or to Miami with you, Mrs. Wolczek. I think his seeing the two of you together has been therapeutic. Notice how pleased he is as he looks at you now."

Leo felt blessed to have such perfectly matched parents. He was happy to note that his father's two blue eyes canceled out his mother's two blue eyes and that his dad's black oxford shoes canceled out his mom's black pumps and the tin of chocolate chip cookies that his mom brought canceled out the bag of Famous Amos chocolate chip cookies that his dad had brought.

After seeing how therapeutic their conjoint visit was, Leo's mother and father, after a whispered conversation, informed the doctor they had decided not to leave town but to reunite and spend as much time as needed working with the doctor to help their son become whole again.

It took three months before Leo tossed his mottled-covered workbooks into a trash bin.

CHAPTER TWENTY-FIVE

Formula or Bust!

Having just come from a screening of "Shock & Awe," an important and informative film that my son Rob directed and starred in, I recalled what a long and circuitous road he took to get to where he is today. My thoughts went back to when this six-foot-four bearded man was a six-week old baby boy who weighed but ten pounds. At that time I was starring in the 1947 musical "Call Me Mister" and was living with my wife, Estelle, and our newborn in a small Chicago apartment. When Robbie was born, our obstetrician recommended that, for his health and growth, we purchase a regimen of formulas from the local pharmacy.

At that time there was a book entitled "The Rights of Infants."

The classic guide to "mothering" for the enrichment of your baby's emotional and physical development.

From its author, Margaret Ribble, we learned that for the first year of a baby's life there is no better nutrition than mother's milk.

Little Robbie was a happy, smiley baby who was being breast fed multiple times a day. As young parents we worried about his weight and wondered about his getting enough nutrition. From the book we learned that pediatricians, by adjusting the baby's daily formula, were making themselves indispensable. These doctors were charging fees that they would otherwise not be earning if the babies were breast fed.

To learn if there was something our baby was lacking, we contacted Dr. Brodsky, an unprepossessing pediatrician whose office was in an old wood-frame house in a working class neighborhood.

"So," he asked, "what can I do for you?"

"Well, doctor, my wife and I were wondering if our baby was getting a proper amount of nutrition."

"And why do you ask that?"

"We don't know if he's getting enough to eat."

"Mr. Reiner, tell me... do you have food in the house?"

"Of course."

"And Mrs. Reiner, are you eating three meals a day?"

"Oh yes, but even so, he seems rather skinny..."

"That is none of your business. If you have a skinny baby, you love a skinny baby, if you have a fat baby, you love a fat baby. Now, tell me how many times a day do you feed him?"

"Every few hours... on demand."

"And what are you feeding him?"

"I'm nursing him..."

"Ah, so he's being breast fed." the doctor sighed and smiled. "Go home, Mrs. Reiner, as I always tell my patients,

'Mother's milk is not only the perfect nutrition but it comes in such cute containers."

I am in the process of starting a new novel and in looking for an inspiration I wondered what inspired Alexander Dumas to write one of my all-time favorite novels, "The Count of Monte Cristo."

So far, I have come up with the following:

"Lovely Lady Ashcroft"

CHAPTER TWENTY-SIX

Loveless Lady Ashcroft
CHAPTER ONE

The first time Lydia Langford became aware of the existence of the man who was the spitting image of a young Cary Grant was when her friend Arlene, who was seated four seats to her left, whispered on her cell phone, "Lydia, don't look up, just keep reading your book! There is a verrry good looking gent staring at you- and has been for the past few minutes. He is sitting directly opposite you and right now he is checking out your legs. Why did you uncross them!? Don't answer–you did right–they look better that way. Now that you've lowered your book, he is checking out your bosom. I think he's smiling... unless that's how his lips are in repose. Go back to reading... no, no then you couldn't be talking on the phone–just close your eyes and I'll keep you posted."

Arlene had been checking the behavior of this handsome devil since he had entered at the last stop and sat opposite Lydia. Lydia did not see him arrive, as she was engrossed in reading her trashy novel, "Lovely Lady Ashcroft." Arlene wondered why this well dressed, drop dead handsome leading man was using the subway as his mode of transportation.

'Did the studio forget to send a limo,' she thought, 'or did Adonis' limo break down or did the pouring rain make taxis unavailable? What other reason could there be for a movie star to be riding in a subway?'

Arlene then looked about for the hidden camera and thought, 'Somebody must be photographing him for a film they're shooting.'

"Arlene," Lydia whispered into her cell phone, "what's he doing now?"

"He's still staring at you-only more intently. Oh, Lydia!"

"What 'Oh Lydia?' Should I look up?"

"Not unless you want to bat your beautiful hazel eyes. Mr. Movie Star is holding a small camera and it looks like he's going take a photo of you–do you want that?"

Before Arlene could answer, 'Mr. Movie Star' stood up, crossed to Lydia and in a British accented voice that befit his looks, he said,

"I'm sorry to interrupt, but may I ask you a question?"

"Sure," Lydia answered quickly, then into her cell phone said, "I'll call you back–mother."

The sight of Lydia and Arlene putting their cell phones away in tandem brought a knowing smile to the man's dimpled cheeks.

"Your friend," he asked, warmly, "called and told you I was staring at you, didn't she?"

"She did," Lydia admitted sheepishly. "You said that you wanted to ask me a question?"

"Actually two questions. The first was, 'would you mind my taking a photo of you?'"

"Well, I don't know-uh, what's the second question?"

"It's about the book you were reading and seemed to be enjoying."

"Loveless Lady Ashcroft?" she said, apologetically. "Oh, it's just something I picked up at the newsstand."

"Are you enjoying it?"

"Well, yes—I guess I am—it's not great literature... some people might consider it trashy."

"Do you consider it trashy, Miss...?"

"Langer, Lydia Langer," she offered, smiling. "Not trashy—perhaps overly romantic is a more apt description. It's a fairly well written autobiography of this fictional character, Lady Ashcroft, a sort of loose woman. Why are you so interested, Mr. Uh?"

"Ashcroft, Philip Ashcroft."

"Ashcroft? You have the same name as the character in this book?"

"Yes, and by the way, this book is not fiction."

"You mean Lady Ashcroft is a real person?"

"As real as was Lady Andrea Dreiser, who was not a loose woman but a politically active one and was, I am proud to say, my maternal Grandmother."

"Really?"

"Really! And now, Miss Langer, would you be so kind as to answer my first question?"

"Your first question? Oh yes... why are you interested in taking a photo of me?"

"Because you remind me of Lady Dreiser..."

"I remind you of your grandmother...?"

"In many ways, the least being the astonishing physical resemblance."

With that, Philip Ashcroft retrieved his wallet, took from it a small photo, which he handed to her. An apprehensive Lydia glanced at it and exploded, "Oh my God!"

"Except for the hairdo," she giggled, "we could be twins!"

"Precisely the reason I must take that photo of you!"

"Please be my guest, and make a duplicate of your Grandmother's photo, "Lydia ordered as she waved at her smiling friend Arlene, "I want to show it to my friend... and my parents!"

"Will do and, if you don't object, I'd like to take as many as I can..."

"Snap away! What are you going to do with them?"

"Show them to the Studios."

"What studios?"

"All of them... Warner Brothers, The Weinstein Brothers, Universal, MGM, Fox, both Stevens, Spielberg and Soderbergh, and Mel Brooks' Brooksfilms."

"Do you have a producer and director in mind?"

"Yes, me! To protect my property, I plan to do both. Miss Langer, have you ever acted?"

"Well, yes I have," she admitted, blushing, "but not professionally. In high school I understudied the lead role in 'Kiss Me Kate'... and in an English class I, and Ken Lebow, my best friend Sally's boyfriend, did the balcony scene from "Romeo and Juliet." It was a disaster... I lost both my best friend Sally and any interest in having a career in the theater."

"Well, Miss Langer, perhaps fate has decreed that you resuscitate your career."

"How so?"

"Had it not been raining and had my car not been in the shop for repairs, I would not have been riding in a subway and found my "Lovely Lady Ashcroft.""

NOTE: *As Franz Schubert's Eighth Symphony was unfinished, so is my "Loveless Lady Ashcroft" unfinished.*

CHAPTER TWENTY-SEVEN

Atheist Carl Commonman Helps
The Almighty Become Almightier

In olden days man's struggle to exist was monumental, and in his quest for help, he started to pray. To bring him food and comfort, it is known that he prayed to rocks, to conch shells, to trees and to the stars. Throughout history there has always been one individual, smarter than the rest, who thought deeply about his existence, and it was he who invented a supreme being who would have the answers for survival. It was he who, in prehistoric times, thought to follow the wolves and feed off the carcasses that the predators left behind.

Many centuries later it was a man called Moses who wrote of a supreme being who lived in the sky above who had the power to answer man's prayers. On a desert mountain, Mt. Sinai, amid thunderclaps, Moses heard the voice of God and chiseled God's ten laws on stone tablets.

If, God told him, man follows my laws he would, after death, be allowed to enter the Kingdom of Heaven. It is not unlikely that the lightning and thunderclaps Moses heard when inscribing the tablets suggested that God might very well be speaking to him.

For the most part, the supplicants' prayers were not answered. They received neither food, shelter nor protection from marauding packs of vicious animals. The Rabbis and wisemen at the time convinced their followers that, after death, they would receive their just rewards in Heaven.

This brings me to a premise I wrote about in one of my best and least appreciated books, "Just Desserts."

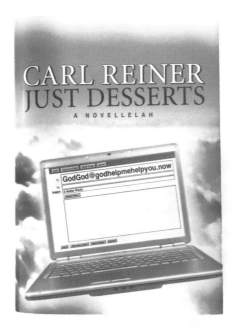

In it, I wrote about Man getting his 'just desserts' on earth. If he did a good deed, the world should know about it and could applaud him for it. If he did an incivility, the world would know that too, and he'd be derided for it. This is illustrated by a scene on a busy New York street where an elderly couple hails a cab. As they open the door to get into it, a thoughtless man pushes past them and commandeers their cab. God, making his magic, has the cab door fly open and the thoughtless man fly out of the cab and land against the front door of an apartment building.

"Wha... wha... what just happened?" the hapless man croaked.

"What shoulda happened," The doorman shouted, "you got yanked outa that old couple's cab."

When the man stood up and tried to walk, God's comeuppance came further into play. Each step he took was accompanied by a high hop into the air, each hop moving him but a half-inch forward. To get from the front door to the curbside he had to hop one-hundred times. This outlandish behavior caused a crowd to gather, a crowd who learned the penalty for a man's incivil behavior.

To many of the onlookers he looked very much like this 1919 tabloid news photo of a gentleman bouncing on a Pogo Stick.

CHAPTER TWENTY-EIGHT

Charlie & The President

The most gratifying thing about receiving the Mark Twain Prize was the opportunity it gave me to sing the praises of my brother, Charlie, who prodded me to become an actor. I was also able to thank my other benefactor, Franklin D. Roosevelt, who created the WPA, which offered free classes for aspiring actors. Not only were my wife, children and grandchildren present, but my brother, Charlie, who four months earlier had been told that he had but a few weeks to live.

Charlie had been in a hospice program that was set up in his bedroom, and would have continued with it had not his children, Richard and Elaine, convinced him to try the new cancer drugs that, if effective, would give him more time... time they would appreciate having with him.

He had told me how sorry and disappointed he was that he would not be able to travel to Washington for the October 24 award ceremony. I assured him that he would see the show before the rest of the country. It was not scheduled to be aired until the following February, but I promised to send him a tape as soon as it was edited.

I would call him at his home in Atlanta and get daily updates on his condition from his wife, Ilse, a marvel of a woman and, from his caring children, Ritchie and Elaine. The drugs seemed to be working and had helped Charlie to get several weeks past his originally projected expiration date.

A month before the award show, the first in a series of minor miracles started with a call.

"Carl, guess where I am?" he asked playfully.

"In the toilet emptying your catheter bag?" I joked.

It may seem indelicate of me to have made that remark, but those are the things you say when you check in every day for a medical update. There were days of elation when the blood level in his urine was down, but there were other days when the news was less heartening. On this day, there was excitement in his voice.

"No, I'm not in the toilet!" he answered smugly, "I am in a tuxedo rental store, and in case I can make it, I'm getting fitted for a tux to wear at that Mark Twain thing."

And three weeks later, there he was in the family box of the Kennedy Center concert hall, sitting in a wheelchair, wearing his rented "in-case-I-can-make-it tuxedo," and smiling down at me.

Not only did he "make it" to the event but he "made it" to the party afterward, holding court at a table where, for hours, he chatted, laughed, and shmoozed with what seemed like every member of the audience.

The event was a theatrical highlight for both of us. I appreciated that all of my very good friends and close acquaintances not only showed up but went onstage and said nice things about me and, more importantly, got big laughs saying them. One memory that is still very much alive for me was not the event itself but an unexpected aftermath. Our producer, Mark Krantz informed me that the President's appointment secretary had called to invite us to the White House. President Clinton wished to meet and greet our group and personally present me with the Mark Twain Prize.

The following morning, in the Oval Office, President Clinton greeted my brother, Charlie, his wife Ilse, my wife Estelle, me, our daughter Annie, our son Rob, his wife Michele, and their children, Jake, Nick, and Romy; our son Lucas, his wife Maude and their daughters, Livia and Dia Rose, my nephew, George Shapiro, his wife Diane, my niece Elaine, my nephew Richard, his wife Helene and their children, Rachel and Max.

On stage, in good spirits, were my dear show biz compadres, Dick Van Dyke, Mary Tyler Moore, Rob Reiner, Jerry Seinfeld, Joy Behar and Steve Martin. Their talent, wit, and gracious presence helped make the show a roaring success.

A word about these stars and the guilt I felt for allowing the show's producers to intrude on their busy lives by asking them to fly across the continent just to help me receive a prize. It is only because Mark Twain was everbody's hero that I managed to exorcize my guilt.

As I looked over at Charlie, I thought, '*The son-of-a-gun beat the odds, or at least improved them enough to be with us on this day.*'

When President Clinton arrived, we were all invited into the Oval Office to meet and be photographed with him. He was as charming and gracious as everyone who has ever met him said he was. After the President chatted with each one of my family and friends, the official White House photographer took this precious shot of him handing me this bronze bust of Mark Twain.

To Carl Reiner
Congratulations, *Bill Clinton*

When I introduced the President to my brother, I mentioned that in WWII, Charlie was one of the Army's first inductees.

Here we see President Roosevelt standing by, as Henry Stimson, the Secretary of War, drew numbers from a glass bowl. The first was #158, the number my brother and 6,175 others held. They were the first draftees who were called up to serve.

I told President Clinton about my brother being in eleven major battles, his first being the invasion of North Africa in 1942, where he was a member of an anti-tank corps.

Our tanks were no match for stopping the Nazis' massive, iron-clad, Panzer tanks.

His last major battle–the D-Day invasion of Normandy on June 6, 1944 and for which he had been awarded a Bronze Star.

President Clinton shook Charlie's hand warmly, and to bring himself down to Charlie's wheel-chair level, sat on the corner of his desk.

For the next fifteen minutes Charlie and the President chatted about that fateful day, and I was amazed at one exchange they had. Charlie mentioned that his outfit did not make the initial landing on Omaha Beach because the Supreme Allied Command had decided that my brother's division were battle weary after having been in ten major campaigns.

Instead of invading Omaha Beach, they were given a four day respite before landing on Utah Beach.

The President surprised Charlie by asking, "If I'm not mistaken, your outfit took both Ste. Marie l'Eglise and St. Malo."

"Yes," Charlie answered, "how did you know that?"

"I read a lot," said the President, smiling.

During the first ten minutes, President Clinton and Corporal Reiner were having a spirited conversation, when a White House aide reminded the President that his helicopter was on the front lawn ready to fly him to New York. The President smiled, said he would be out in a few minutes, and turned his attention back to my brother.

"Charlie," he asked, "did you get to revisit Normandy last month for the fiftieth anniversary of D-Day?"

Charlie said that he did not.

A lot of things have been said and written about President Clinton, some true, some false, some flattering, some derogatory, some deserved, some not, but that afternoon I was privy to discover something about President Clinton that I am pleased to pass on.

He described that 50th Anniversary of D-Day as being an extraordinarily moving and emotional one for him. He talked about an old friend from his hometown who had accompanied him to the site on which he had stood fifty years earlier. This gentleman, President Clinton said, was one of the many courageous soldiers who, a half century ago, clawed his way up the Normandy slopes to engage the enemy. The President related how his friend stood next to him and scanned the thousands of white headstones marking the plots where thousands of our boys were laid to rest.

"After a long moment," the President said, "my friend pointed to a bluff nearby, and quietly said, 'That's the spot where I saw a bomb hit my brother and blow him to pieces.' He then looked about," the President continued, "and with tears welling up in his eyes, the old man pointed to another area on the hill, and said, 'And over there, a few moments later, I saw my other brother get blown away.'

"The old gent," Clinton continued, "started to cry like a baby, and it got to me. I couldn't hold back. I just let go and cried with him."

While he was relating this to Charlie, the President's voice cracked and his eyes filled with tears. An aide approached to remind him that the helicopter was waiting. Before leaving, President Clinton had a few more words for Charlie that I did not hear. He shook his hand, said a blanket good-bye to our family and friends and left. His eyes were still damp when he shook my hand, and I thought about all the jokes and comments his detractors had made about his use of the phrase, "I feel your pain." He might have overused that phrase, but that day, I saw, firsthand and up close, a man who had the compassion and the capacity to actually feel someone else's pain.

That day, on October 25 of the year 2000, all of us returned from whence we came, some to New York, some to Los Angeles, and Charlie, Ilse, and their daughter to their home in Atlanta, Georgia.

For the next four months, Charlie and I spoke by phone every day and we discussed his physical condition, the state of the world, and the screwed-up presidential election. Often, we would reminisce about our parents, who had left us many years ago. We thought of how much they would have enjoyed getting the dozens of wonderful photos of President Clinton posing with members of our family. We pictured our mother, Bessie, stuffing those photos in her purse, going to The Bronx's Crotona Park, sitting down on "her bench" and showing off those pictures to all of her friends, acquaintances, and unsuspecting passersby. Charlie and I agreed that it was a miracle of miracles that he was able to make that trip and be at the show. He worried that he might not be around to see it aired. It was to be televised four months hence on the 28th of February.

With the help of his wife and his daughter, caring nurses, and modern medicines, it looked as though he would get to see himself at the Kennedy Center. A couple of days before the show aired, I called to tell him that I had sent a tape of the show by Federal Express so he could play it at his leisure, and he was happy about that. He was also very happy to report that he was feeling wonderful.

"Guess what I did today?" he said, sounding the way he did when he called me from the tuxedo rental store, "I got out of bed, slipped into my shoes, and went outside for a walk."

He had, a couple of months earlier, managed to take a short walk and retrieve the mail from their curbside mailbox. "Charlie, you're kidding! You actually felt well enough to walk to the mailbox?"

"Not to the mailbox," he said proudly, "to the street. I walked on the road, and without my cane. I went for about half a mile."

"That's a long walk."

"You're telling me? I was too tired to walk back!"

"How did you get back?"

"Elaine picked me up with the car . . . I was pooped!"

Incredible as it seemed, I believed him, I guess because I wanted to believe that he was getting better.

A few minutes later when I spoke with Ilse and my niece, Elaine, they told me that the half-mile walk was in his mind.

"But," I argued, "he sounds exactly like himself!"

They explained that he went in and out of fantasy, and that he got very tired and went to sleep very early every night. They were glad that the tape of the show was coming the following morning, because mornings were when he was most alert. They didn't think he would be able to stay awake until nine o'clock to see it on television.

Charlie did not get to see himself on tape or on television. He didn't get to see himself looking handsome in his rented tuxedo or again hear all the lovely things I was moved to say about him. He passed away early that morning.

On March 4, 2001, at Arlington National Cemetery, our family witnessed Cpl. Reiner's military funeral with full honors, his name engraved on a Niche Wall plaque...

...and a Color Guard honoring him with a 21 gun salute.

Charlie left us when he was eighty-two... and he is still sorely missed.

CHAPTER TWENTY-NINE

Seeing The Dick Van Dyke Show In Color

I've said it before and I will say it again:

Whenever asked of which show I am most proud of having been a part, I always answer "Hands down, The Dick Van Dyke Show."

I would be remiss if I did not include photos of two shows that CBS chose to air last Sunday, both written by Bill Persky and Sam Denoff. Two things stood out, one, seeing it in living color and, two, hearing from friends and fans that the show continues to be both entertaining and current. These stills, in living color, are accurate. In the 1960's an enterprising photographer had taken color shots of the sets and of the actors. Following are images taken from the episode "That's My Boy."

Morey Amsterdam & Rosemarie   Mary & Dick

Richard Deacon   Jerry Paris & Ann Morgan Guilbert

Greg Morris & Mimi Dillard

Below are photos from a show entitled "Coast to Coast Big Mouth" of which I am very fond.

Here is Laura Petrie apologizing to Alan Brady for disclosing that he wears a toupee.

And here is Alan Brady
not accepting her apology.

Laura acknowledging what irreparable damage she has done to Alan Brady's public persona.

I am particularly fond of this show because it enabled Alan Brady to deliver this line of dialogue to his toupees:

"Fellas, there she is! There's the little lady who put you out of business."

From 1970-1977 Mary Tyler Moore as Mary Richards in "The Mary Tyler Moore Show" gracefully tossed her hat in the air.

On January 26th Mary Tyler Moore, who turned the world on with her smile, left a mutitude of mourners when she passed away the age of 80.

When thinking about Mary Tyler Moore's passing away at 80 I realized how lucky I am. As Mel Brooks remarked I am, "Too Busy To Die."

I press on but I do have qualms about the two following chapters. I wasn't sure whether they are interesting enough but decided to let you, my readers, judge whether or not they are worthy of inclusion. If your response is negative, these stories will not appear in the second printing of this book.

CHAPTER THIRTY

Timothy & Dimothy

This morning while shaving, I started to have a conversation with myself. I rushed to record what may become a fascinating play and gave it the above title.

Cast of characters:
-Timothy: Brainy, British Duke. (Tim)
-Dimothy: Brainless, Bronx Dude. (Dim)

These men are cousins who have recently inherited billions... not dollars, Euros!

Scene 1:

A tastefully decorated bedroom. Dim is sound asleep. Tim enters. He taps Dim's forehead.

Tim: Dim, you awake?
Dim: I dunno.
Tim: You are. You spoke to me.
Dim: What'd I say?
Tim: I don't know.
Dim: Weren't ya lis'ning?
Tim: You were mumbling.
Dim: What'd I mumble?
Tim: I dunno.
Dim: Ya did'n unnerstan?
Tim: (*wearily*) I understood. I heard you.
Dim: Why d'ya wake me?
Tim: Because there are problems.
Dim: What kinda problems?
Tim: Serious ones, I dare say.
Dim: Okay, I dare ya! Say'em.
Tim: Dim, its about our future.
Dim: Our future? I just met ya—t'ree days ago.

Tim: I know.

Dim: You come t'me wit a bullshit story...

Tim: A true story!

Dim: You say a relative croaked?

Tim: Passed... leaving us some money.

Dim: Yeah! Ya said a shit load of bucks.

Tim: A **ship** load of Euros and I'm worried.

Dim: Whatcha worried about?

Tim: Your future.

Dim: Whad about my future?

Tim: It's at stake!

Dim: Steak? Like a rib-eye?

Tim: No. Like legacy and longevity.

Dim: Talk English, shmucko!

Tim: To attain longevity, only surgery can help you.

Dim: Help me what?

Tim: We'll continue this discussion in transit.

Dim: Who's getting transitted?

Tim: We are. The ambulance driver awaits curbside.

Dim: What da hell for?

Tim: To drive us.

Dim: Where the fuck to?

Tim: To Mount Sinai-Presbyterian.

Dim: Hey dat's a friggin' hospital!

Tim: It is! The city's finest facility.

Dim: Is dis some sicko joke?

Tim: It is no joke!

Dim: Whadda you, a friggin' prankster?

Tim: It's hardly a prank!

Dim: Then what da fuck is it?

Tim: There's no need for vulgarity.

Dim: What d'fuck's up your ass?

Tim: Same as yours, major trouble.

Dim: You're full of crap!

Tim: Precisely, and impacted.

Dim: So take an enema!

Tim: That my dilemma!

Dim: An enema's your dilemena?
Tim: **Dilemma** –yours and mine.
Dim: Mine!? What' d'hell you smokin'?
Tim: Dim, the ambulance that awaits us...
Dim: ...from dat Cyanide Perspreterian?
Tim: Sinai Presbyterian.
Dim: And why're we goin' dere?
Tim: To undergo a procedure.
Dim: I don't need no procedure.
Tim: You do. We do.
Dim: What's wid dis we?
Tim: We are related.
Dim: Yeah! Like thirtieth cousins.
Tim: Not thirtieth–third!
Dim: This is bullshit.
Tim: Not according to Doctor Layton.
Dim: Who's dat?
Tim: Our only hope.
Dim: For what?
Tim: For staying alive.
Dim: Who's dying?
Tim: We are, unless Dr. Layton successfully transplants
       half of your kidney in me and half of my liver in you.
Dim:Why the fuck we wanna do that?
Tim: To save us from perishing from the rare disease
       Peristinotic Symbiotic Duadonic Flaguletum.
Dim: How much is this gonna cost?
Tim: Not a cent. It's experimental. First time it's being attempted.
Dim: Ok, I'm in. Do we get ice cream after da operation?
Tim: I'm sure we will.
Dim: Tell'em I want two scoops--rocky road and butter pecan.

Note: *The operation was a success but the patients died of tainted ice cream.*

CHAPTER THIRTY-ONE

After writing a playful playette, I was inspired to write a novel novelette.

My Very Novel New Novelette

"What's novel about this novelette?"
"Its title for one."
"My Very Novel New Novelette?"
"Does it not intrigue you?"
"Just enough to be curious."
"That was my proudest hope."
"My curiosity makes you proud?"
"Among other things."
"What other things?"
"Its structure, for one."
"What about its structure?"
"Haven't you noticed?"
"Noticed what??"
"The five word sentences."
"Five word sentences is stupid!"
"Maybe, but also a boon."
"A boon to whom?"
"Busy people, lazy people.
"What's the novel's first sentence?"
"Where am I?"
"The second sentence?"
"How did I get here?"
"And the third sentence?"
"Who are you, madame?"
"Who is she?"
"Aha, you are intrigued."
"Not intrigued, just interested, continue."
My name is Carole."
"Carole what?"
"Guess!"

"Burnett, Lombard?"
"Neither, keep guessing!"
"Lewis?"
"Who's Carroll Lewis?"
"Alice In Wonderland's author."
"That's Lewis Carroll."
"So it is, keep going."
"King Carol of Roumania?"
"Don't be sarcastic."
"How should I be?"
"Try saccharine or sachramose."
"Don't you mean lachrymose?"
"I don't know that word."
"All bonafide novelists do."
"I am a bonafried novelist!"
"You admit being a drunk?"
"You do nothing but cod!"
"It 'carp,' not cod."
"Go frig yourself!"
"Don't you mean fuck myself!"
"Thou hast said it, shmucko!"
"I'm proud of this work."
"Why?"
"Because of it's originality."
"What makes it original?"
"For one, its length."
"How long will it be?"
"Two more sentences."
"Two more sentences?"
"Yes, that and this one."

THE END

CHAPTER THIRTY-TWO

Creation

He wondered how long he would have to stare at a blank piece of paper before a usable idea came to him.

"Where to begin? What to say?"

"Start writing," he instructed himself, "It will come."

He placed his hand on the scroll and was pleased to see the letter **N** appear.

That night he went to bed happy, knowing that he had done a full and fruitful day's work.

The following day was even more productive. He had sat looking at the **N** for half a day, when an **E** appeared on his parchment, then, miraculously, an **M**, then another **E**, then an **S**, an **I** and another **S** and stared at what his right hand had writ, **NEMESIS**. "No, no, no," he mumbled, "this will not do!" With a quick stroke of his sharpened reed, he changed the **N** to a **G** and read aloud, "**GEMISIS**." His natural writer's instinct told him that what he had writ was good, but that a thoughtful rewrite would make it better.

The following morning he awoke at dawn and ran to his scroll. His brain was afire! He retrieved what he had written–**GEMISIS**, quickly replaced the **M** with an **N** and slowly articulated the world **GENESIS**. "Ah, a good beginning," he mused, "a very good beginning." He read the word aloud many times that day and thought, '*This could turn out to be a good book. A Good Book??* **Yes! Yes! Yes... And so it came to pass**..........................:

"THE GOOD BOOK"

By
THE ALMIGHTY

January 1, 0000

CHAPTER THIRTY-THREE

The Almighty

There are fifteen things about The Almighty that are never mentioned anywhere. I personally know that:

- He has a chronic back condition.
- His knee joints ache.
- He's allergic to shellfish and mustard.
- His prostate is moderately enlarged.
- He often sings off-key.
- He hates wars but can't think of a way to stop them.
- He loves to check out a woman's legs as she passes by.
- He is upset by the unfair distribution of wealth.
- He loves to laugh.
- He gets goosebumps when a great tenor hits a high C.
- He hates that comedies rarely, if ever, win Oscars.
- He loves sushi, especially Unagi.
- He hates talking to anyone wearing a tongue ring.
- He would like to replace the Ten Commandments.
  with One Commandment that covers everything:
  Thou Shall Not Hurt Anybody.

How do I know these things about God?

I am man and I was told that He created me in His image.

Now what do I do???

What you do is
start a new book and call it:

"Pay Dirt or Just Dirt."

Other works by Carl Reiner:

Enter Laughing

The 2000 Year Old Man:
The Complete History

All Kinds of Love

Continue Laughing

The 2000 Year Old Man in
the Year 2000: The Book

How Paul Robeson Saved My Life
And Other Mostly Happy Stories

My Anecdotal Life

NNNNN

Just Desserts: A Novellelah

I Remember Me

I Just Remembered

What I Forgot To Remember

Why and When The Dick Van Dyke Show Was Born

Carl Reiner, Now You're Ninety-Four

Children's books by Carl Reiner:

Tell Me A Scary Story
But Not Too Scary!

The 2000 Year Old Man
Goes To School

Tell Me Another Scary Story
But Not Too Scary!

Tell Me A Silly Story

Too Scared To Scream

The Secret Treasure Of Tahka Paka

You Say God Bless You
For Sneezing & Farting

Broadway Play by Carl Reiner:

Something Different